INFORMATION TECHNOLOGY IN 21ST CENTURY

INFORMATION TECHNOLOGY IN 21ST CENTURY

(In 9 Volumes)

DIMENSIONS OF INFORMATION TECHNOLOGY ISSUES

(Volume 9)

PROF. RAMESH CHANDRA

Vice-Chancellor, Bundelkhand University, Jhansi (U.P.)

Publication

KALPAZ PUBLICATIONS

DELHI–110052

INFORMATION TECHNOLOGY IN 21ST CENTURY
Dimension of Information Technology Issues
(Information Technolgy)

Rs. 8000 (Set)
Rs. 900 (each volume)

ISBN: 81-7835-158-7 (Set)
ISBN: 81-7835-167-6 (Vol. 9)

Published in 2003 in India by
Kalpaz Publications
C-30, Satyawati Nagar
Delhi-110052
E-mail: kalpaz@hotmail.com

Laser Typesetting at: A.S. Printers
Printed at: Chawla Offset Printers, Delhi

Preface

The twentieth century has witnessed an exciting and exhaustive explosion in the arena of information amplification. The computers and internet are developed to such a situation that they became the core of the information technology activities. In many instances, they can be regarded as synonymous to information technology in the modern era. The widespread availability of global information systems carries with it the promise for the generation and sharing of information at a degree of complexity and pervasiveness that was unimaginable until recently.

The cyber networking allow citizens of a community to connect to the global computer communication network and provide them with the facility to communicate with other members of their own community and with the world. Already, information is being posted on the 'net' that would otherwise only be available to a restricted group, if its existence were known at all. Unlike transmission programmes consisting of sounds or images that are produced solely for communication to the public in sequence and as a unit, digital information is inherently malleable. Information expressed as sequences of binary digits may be accessed interactively, data streams from widely distributed sources may be intermingled, and new works dynamically generated and processed.

While information society promises to enhance social and economic well being it also threatens some core issues such as, violation of rights, privacy, etc. Here comes the need to regulate the cyber activity, but the regulation of the activities of cyber space is not at all easy. Laws relating to broadcasting media, data protection, evidence, contract, tort, and intellectual property—all have a role to play, as do provisions of civil and criminal law.

This book describes the dimensions of revolutionary changes taking place in the field of information and communication technologies. This will certainly prove highly useful for students and teachers in the field of information science.

Editor

Contents

1

Introduction

Work has been going forward on the development of a frame of reference for locating and invoking digital information services and objects over communication systems and pathways having computational capabilities. An important concept in this context is the notion of a 'digital object' as a set of sequences of bits, including a unique identifier for the object called a 'handle'. A digital object may incorporate digital works and other digital information in which copyright, patent, trade secret and other rights or interests are claimed, although this need not always be the case. To take full advantage of the global information infrastructure, it is helpful for a commercial enterprise to develop a flexible terminology for thinking about digital information from a copyright perspective; in this regard, the concept of 'digital work' is suggested. Clearance of rights and interests in connection with the 'contents' of digital objects may be treated separately from compliance with procedures for accessing digital objects viewed as entities that incorporate and identify contents. A suggested legal framework is discussed.

Often, a period of intellectual progress is stimulated by a marked technical advance. It is widely recognized that the printing press was such a development. Whereas, before this invention, only a few books were laboriously produced and available to the public, the printing press opened the doors for a sharing of information to a much larger reading public. While there is certainly disagreement on the quality of scholarship evident in many works structured as books and published in printed form, there is little doubt that this new procedure for communicating ideas had a major impact on civilization. Other data structures also emerged to take advantage of the capabilities of the printing press such as newspapers, monographs, and journals.

In this century, radio and television technology ushered in a yet more diversified medium of communication. In addition to expressing ideas with printed text and illustrations, information could be widely shared in a dynamic form consisting of a series of related sounds and images. While the data structure understood as a "book" played (and continues to play) a lead role in the print- on-paper world, a unifying structure, known as the transmission program developed to facilitate the origination and transmission of information in the broadcast, cable and satellite communications industries.

This unit for organizing and identifying information has generally been regulated under communications and trade laws, but it also has implications for the application of copyright law in a communications environment. For example, provision was made in the North American Free Trade Agreement (NAFTA) for protection of "encrypted program-carrying satellite signals."

Over the last decade, there has been substantial growth in public perception and use of computer networking capabilities for the creation and dissemination of copyright works. Of particular note is the emergence of the Internet. This phenomenon is not a unique situation in the history of intellectual progress. It has been a distinguishing feature of human potential to challenge existing assumptions, to reconceptualize given knowledge, and to generate diverse informational materials and artifacts for entertainment, educational, industrial and other purposes. Technology has simply helped to accelerate the process.

The widespread availability of global information systems like the Internet carries with it the promise for the generation and sharing of information at a degree of complexity and pervasiveness that was unimaginable until recently. Already, information is being posted on the "Net" that would otherwise only be available to a restricted group, if its existence were known at all. Unlike transmission programs consisting of sounds or images that are produced solely for communication to the public in sequence and as a unit, digital information is inherently malleable. Information expressed as sequences of binary digits (or bits) may be accessed interactively, data streams from widely distributed sources may be intermingled, and new works dynamically generated and processed.

There is a growing perception in the research community, and, increasingly, by leaders in copyright-dependent industries, that data structures should be developed to enable the organization and identification of units of digital information for purposes of copyright protection in a network environment. Efforts in this direction are well underway. Of particular note, is a framework under development that will enable copyright works and other information resources, once configured as "digital objects," to be reproduced, stored, accessed and disseminated over computer networks in this new form of data structure. This architecture grew out of a program organized and led by the Corporation for National Research Initiatives (CNRI) under the sponsorship of the U.S. Defense Advanced Research Projects Agency, and with the active participation of the U.S. Copyright Office of the Library of Congress. Fundamental aspects of this information infrastructure were described by Robert Kahn and Robert Wilensky.

The notion of "digital objects" (sometimes referred to as packages, containers, or, more generally, structured bit sequences) and their supporting technologies has emerged as a focus of experimentation. In this context, the concept of a digital object is defined simply as a set of sequences of bits, which contains "typed data" (to allow the sequences to be interpreted), and includes a unique identifier for the object known as a "handle" (or, in certain instances, a "DOI").

The digital object is intended to be a generic means of structuring information in the digital world. A digital object may incorporate information in which copyright, patent, trade secret or other rights or interests may be claimed, although this need not always be the case.

Digital objects may be deposited and stored in a network-based computer system called a "repository" for possible subsequent access. Repositories may be operated in a variety of ways, spanning the range from individual storage depots--to bulletin boards--to broadcast stations on the Internet. From a copyright perspective, it is important to stress that a "handle" identifies a particular logical entity, i.e., a data structure in which a work or other information has been embodied, but not the underlying information itself.

A unique and important attribute of a digital object embodying a copyright work is the capability of the object to incorporate, in what is termed its "metadata," conditions for accessing the digital object and/or its underlying content, or an indicator to where such information may be available. The digital object may also enable a negotiation to take place where a user wishes to go beyond any conditions previously set forth in its metadata. This capability is an essential ingredient to enable and encourage the growth of commerce in copyright works in a digital environment.

The digital object framework is now being implemented in several testbeds, including two at the U.S. Library of Congress and in connection with the Association of American Publishers. A key goal in these efforts is to provide an open architecture which allows the identification and management of access to digital information, where both proprietary and non-proprietary information may be made available in a structured and well-known way with open interfaces, protocols and object structures.

The concept of a digital object as a structured package containing encrypted information may also facilitate the development of flexible and efficient mechanisms for managing rights or interests in a computer network environment. In this context, the keys can be managed and distributed independently from the digital object itself. This capability for managing rights or interests also applies where intelligent agents, structured as digital objects, act on behalf of rightsholders in a network environment to protect works embodied in such objects.

When the United States federal copyright statute was revised about twenty years ago, it restated the two fundamental criteria of copyright protection--"originality" and "fixation in tangible form." From the first U.S. copyright statute which designated only "maps, charts, and books," the copyright law has grown to include new forms of expression as creative and worthy of protection. As noted in the legislative history of the 1976 Copyright Act:

"It makes no difference what the form, manner, or medium of fixation may be--whether it is in words, numbers, notes, sounds, pictures, or any other graphic or symbolic indicia, whether embodied in a physical object in written, printed, photographic, sculptural, punched, magnetic, or any other stable form, and whether it is capable of perception directly or by means of any machine or device 'now known or later developed."

This expansive intent is limited, however, by the wording of the definition of "fixation," where it is specifically provided that a work is "fixed" in a tangible medium of expression when it is embodied in an authorized "copy" or "phonorecord." Generally, a "copy" for these purposes is a material object (other than a phonorecord). This is not just a matter of passing interest in the context of U.S. law. The concept of "fixation" is important since it represents the dividing line between the application of the federal copyright statute and any protection that may be available under State common law or statute.

What it means to be a "copy" also came up at the Diplomatic Conference on Certain Copyright and Neighboring Rights Questions convened by WIPO and held in December 1996. Specifically, the following text appears under the Agreed Statements concerning Articles 6 and 7 of the WIPO Copyright Treaty adopted by the Diplomatic Conference: ". . .the expressions `copies' and `original and copies' being subject to the right of distribution and the right of rental under the said Articles, refer exclusively to fixed copies that can be put into circulation as tangible objects." While the intended meaning of "copies" was thus clarified, the meaning of "original" may require further analysis. In the U.S., an "original" may be deemed to apply to the first fixation of a work in a tangible form; however, many countries extend copyright protection to what are sometimes termed "original" works without a "fixation" requirement.

This topic is particularly interesting to consider where "original works of authorship" for purposes of U.S. law (or what are sometimes termed "original works of the mind" under other bodies of law) are created wholly within a global information system like the Internet, and where there may be no material fixation (or "copy") generated much less distributed. A novel interpretation of materially fixed might include a capability that supports "fixation on demand;" however, there would still be some inherent ambiguity about the status of such works prior to their fixation.

The development of a digital object infrastructure may enable the expansion of copyright protection to accommodate works that are not first fixed in a tangible medium of expression, or, in the case of material such as live broadcasts, that are not recorded simultaneously with their transmission. Introducing the notion of a structured, logical unit, i.e., a "digital object," may better accommodate the emerging capabilities of digital technology, including, in particular, the deployment of such dynamic resources as intelligent agents. This may also avoid the use of ambiguous and oxymoronic terms such as "intangible copies."

In addition to the existing requirement under U.S. law that an original work of authorship be "fixed in a tangible medium of expression" for federal copyright protection to attach, an alternate criteria may prove very useful in a network environment, namely:

"an original work of authorship structured in a persistent, uniquely identifiable medium of expression from which it may be reproduced, perceived, performed or accessed by any device or process for a period of more than transitory duration."

For purposes of this new provision, "structured" may be defined to include digital objects and other equivalent data structures.

While a digital object with its unique persistent identifier thus serves much the same purpose as a material fixation under U.S. law, this concept may also prove of assistance in countries that extend protection without the need for a fixation. A capability of persistently and uniquely identifying a data structure in which copyright works, or performances of works, are embodied may encourage the development of a new marketplace for copyright works in a digital environment.

Questions have been raised about the classification of new creative works like MIDI sequences for purposes of copyright. Are they literary works? Musical works?

Computer programs? Sound recordings? Further, what happens when a network-based repository of such works is accessed on an interactive basis, and the results of such access are disseminated over the Internet? Depending on the nature of the access request, the dissemination may not represent any particular sequence of bits that previously existed in that, or indeed, any repository. This situation is also likely to become increasingly prevalent where complex works such as knowledge-based systems are made commercially available over the Internet to provide advice and guidance on a wide variety of topics.

Many information resources (whether or not configured as digital objects) that are now accessible to the public over the Internet may appear to look and sound like conventional copyright works. Often, the term "multimedia" is applied to these capabilities, as if these resources were simple compilations of several traditional works, such as music, photographs, films or text, to be treated as what might generally be called "data." While it may be appropriate to regard these works as a whole as either computer programs or computer databases, or some combination thereof, a more accurate, comprehensive and flexible terminology to describe this emerging area is needed to reflect the realities of the underlying technology.

Information in digital form (whether of a purely symbolic or numeric character) is a purely conceptual entity; however, it may be represented as a real entity in the form of symbols or numbers fixed in a material object, where it is usually considered a "literary work" for copyright purposes. A committee of the American Bar Association has been exploring whether it might be helpful to establish a subcategory of literary works capable of behavior, to be called "digital works." For discussion purposes, the committee developed a definition of what might be deemed a digital work as follows:

"`Digital works' are literary works consisting of an ordered set of symbols from a discrete alphabet, such as computer programs or knowledge structures, that are capable of behavior when processed."

This is particularly important where a patented process may be involved in the performance of a digital work subject to copyright, or where there may be patents involved in the methods used for structuring data.

If a consensus can be reached on what it means to be a "digital work," it may lead to a better understanding of what occurs from a copyright, patent and communications law perspective when a representation of digital information is mapped into a waveform. Terms such as "digital communication" or "digital transmission" may not be adequate to describe the situation fully. It was the committee's understanding that, strictly speaking, there are only waveforms or "continuous signals" in the real world. A "signal" is meant to be "digital" only in the conceptual sense that it is understood to contain a sequence of discrete symbols or bits.

Any sequence of discrete symbols which corresponds to the expression of certain information may be mapped into one or more continuous waveforms. For purposes of copyright, where this ordered set of symbols is viewed as a "digital work," the mapping of the information into a waveform by any device or process may be viewed as a "performance" of the work. There may be other performances of works that take place, not just at the source, but at the point of reception and within the network itself, where intelligent agents may be tasked with performing various operations. Certain of these performances may be deemed exempt from copyright liability.

Networks and network servers can generally be either active or passive entities in any communications system. As passive entities, they typically serve to communicate bits without essential change from a source to one or more destinations. As active entities, they have the ability to process the information in arbitrary ways. When the information is encrypted at its source, the processing options along the communications pathways are inherently more limited, but it is still possible to perform a limited set of functions within the network such as aggregation, selective filtering and disaggregation. Thus, the extent of copyright liability for any given situation should be based upon the nature of the service being provided. There may be classes of operations performed on digital objects that have only a minimal, if any, impact on any underlying copyright works. While strictly speaking performances, such operations might be deemed to encompass the "distribution" of digital objects embodying copyright works. Complex operations would most likely bring into play the copyright right of public performance.

There may be rules and procedures developed for access to digital objects, or repositories of digital objects, that may overlap and impact in practice any copyright and other rights or interests that apply to the underlying information content. In the context of a digital object infrastructure, there has been some discussion of the notion of "access to perform stated operations on a sequence of bits." Whether, and under what circumstances, such operations should be accommodated under communications laws, and how protection at the digital object level will interact with any copyright, patent, banking, privacy, trade secret, and other rights or interests in an object's contents, is an important area for continued discussion and experimentation. Where a copyright work is configured as an encrypted digital object, a new set of capabilities is introduced having great potential for the management of rights or interests in a network environment, or even for indicating that there are no restrictions placed on access to digital information.

In summary, this chapter has introduced the digital object as a logical structure for organizing information expressed as sequences of bits (like the book or the transmission program in other media). It compares the characteristics of digital objects, i.e., unique persistent identifiers, network accessibility and typed data, to the attributes of fixation in a material object, and shows them to be generally equivalent. In addition, it introduces a notion of a digital work as a literary work that is capable of behavior, and discusses some of the attributes of encrypted digital objects that may bring into play the copyright rights of distribution, as well as public performance, in a network environment.

2

Social Activity in Cyberspace

Internet is a new and unique medium of communication, with emergent conventions and uses that provide lowered communication thresholds and broadened geographical scope. It contains distinctive subcultures that lend themselves to postmodern speculation about its radical deconstructive effect on identity and on culture in general. Turkle's assertion "We are moving from modernist calculation to postmodernist simulation, where the self is a multiple, distributed system," is echoed by that of Stone:

> The identities that emerge from these [Internet] interactions—fragmented, complex, diffracted through the lenses of technology, culture and new technocultural formations—seem to be...more visible as the critters we ourselves are in the process of becoming, here at the close of the mechanical age.

Accounts such as these, based largely on behavior in multi-user domains (muds) and using postmodern psychoanalytic theory as a framework, form a genre of their own in the study of computer-mediated communication.

This genre of research seems to proceed without reference to informing theories developed in other disciplines, specifically information systems and sociology/anthropology, which present accounts of more situated behavior in electronic media. Despite a growing and thoughtful literature developed in these institutionally oriented disciplines, the most publicized views are those expressed in books and papers read by the computing community and the public at large, like Turkle's Life on the screen, and Stone's The war of desire and technology at the close of the mechanical age, just quoted.

These tend to have journalistic appeal based on futurism and radical scenarios, or because they originate within communities unconstrained by prior social theory to project new social scenarios from envisioned changes in technology. Indeed, because of what Dreyfus refers to as "the psychological assumption" of cognition, here extended to the notion of self in society, these authors extrapolate from a set of individual experiences expressed in confessional mode a projection of social change based in Internet communications.

The position taken in this chapter is that Internet does not radically alter the social bases of identity or conventional constraints on social interaction, although it certainly will provide openings for variations based in the new opportunities made available. The issues that arise can be addressed as questions of emerging structures of interaction and reorganization of social boundaries that can occur in any medium of communication.

Theories of talk as coconstructed, situated interaction as well as of technology as a social artifact imply more continuity of Internet behavior with the embodied world than the postmodern view would argue. These writings allow an understanding of the ways Internet is novel, but constrained by inherently social processes through the very orderliness of talk itself and constraints on its production originating in shared understandings, social goals, and accountability.

Missing context for discussion of social issues

It is easy for a provocative book on social issues to be influential in the computing community as well as the general public without being grounded in social theory, because the community is not connected to the dialogue of the social disciplines. Even when part of the theory is well developed and the arguments convincing, problems can arise from this lack of context. The major part of the book explicates important hermeneutic principles and details their application to computing. This section was justifiably acclaimed. It was more effective in communicating the message of hermeneutics to the computer science audience than the prior works of Dreyfus, who was seen as an antagonistic outsider hypercritical of artificial intelligence (AI). By speaking from within the target community, Winograd and Flores were able to put an important message across. The end of the very same book, however, formulates a theory of organizational communication unrelated to the literature on either organizations or interaction. Thus the scholarly excellence of the first half of the book is not reflected in the propositions of the second half on how to incorporate this view into practice. The general audience may fail to note the discontinuity for lack of a grounding in the originating disciplines.

This kind of discontinuity is problematic because it is misleading in a way that would not have been possible within the framework of an ongoing debate in a discipline. In the case of the current works on cyberspace, it is problematic because its audience on the whole lacks the distinctions to differentiate it from other kinds of works on people and culture. Yet it is important to communicate across disciplinary boundaries, because all of the impacts of computing and communications are ultimately social, and their origins are social as well.

The social and technical worlds especially overlap—to the extent that they are constructed as separate—in the field of software engineering, both in terms of methods and of design requirements. It is terribly important that participants in these activities be presented with an adequate view of what it means to define something as "social". But it is not helpful to this purpose and to the general understanding when studies of purportedly social phenomena turn out to be impossible to incorporate into the ongoing practice of adapting technology to society. Therefore, while the deconstructivist psychology of cyberspace is both literate within its scope, exciting to read about, and fascinating to contemplate as a proposition, in the end it disserves the community of people who seriously want to make technologies that are socially situated. It is not based in social theory and is therefore not accountable to the history of discussion of social activity. It runs the risk of marginalizing the social study of computing by making it appear fantastic and unrelated to practical projects that could in fact benefit from a social perspective.

Works in social theory are generally unknown to the computing community in the United States. Because these works are not part of preexisting paradigms of the particular scientific community, it is possible for well-written outlier theories to take hold more easily than would otherwise be the case. Important distinctions are thereby lacking. Dealing with social issues from a psychological perspective is often transparent in this context, that is, seems like a natural, default way to talk about what people do. But psychological theories address issues generated by the study of individuals. Social theories address concerns about collectivities and take them as prior levels of analysis.

This is a critical distinction and one that applies to the current case especially well. For instance, the liberation from a "politically imposed" self is glorified in the postmodern literature we have cited. Yet this same condition has unfavorable and even fatal connotations in the light of that great work of statistical induction, Durkheim's Suicide. We may disagree with Durkheim's theoretical platonism or with the firmness of his construct of suicide. But in defending the thesis that the socially bounded self is a prison, we would have to contend with his methodical march through volumes of historical census data, as he eliminates competing explanations for suicide, to build the convincing case that lack of social boundaries, or anomie, leads people to despair and kill themselves.

The departure from social theory in attempting to explain social phenomena, in Turkle's case, leads to a theoretical radicalism based in deconstructivist philosophy, Lacanian psychoanalytic theory, and neural nets. The work of Stone parallels this line of thinking using additional sources and concerns.

Both claim to base their views in social science but in fact use contemporary psychological and literary theories as a primary basis of argument. The data used in these accounts come from within the target community of computer users that most exemplify the extremes of behavior upheld as social trends. Without social theory and more grounded methods, Internet is plausibly portrayed as fantastic and unreal rather than practical, effective and socially constructed.

The large body of research carried out in the field of information systems and by social scientists involved in technological research can thus be overshadowed by images of technology and society projected through magazines like Wired and popular books like Life on the screen, The war of desire and technology at the close of the mechanical age, and Haraway's Simians, cyborgs and women.

This visibility is the rationale for taking issue with the idea that those works should form a seminal literature for studies of Internet interactions. All this being said, it is an engaging and provocative literature and therefore worth the trouble of examining its premises.

Drawing on data from other kinds of Internet group behaviors, our own and others', as well as on the earlier hermeneutics discussed in Dreyfus we will examine the assumptions embedded in the notion of disembodied selves and transformed culture that Internet purportedly has the power to bring forth.

What Self?

Both Turkle and Stone create a counterpoint between a

traditional notion of "self" that seems to be a psychological definition, and the postmodern diffusion of self as nonlocal and not necessarily embodied.

In the story of constructing identity in the culture of simulation, experiences on the Internet figure prominently, but these experiences can only be understood as part of a larger cultural context. That context is the story of eroding boundaries between the real and the virtual, the animate and the inanimate, the unitary and the multiple self, which is occurring both in advanced scientific fields of research and in the patterns of everyday life.

From scientists trying to create artificial life to children "morphing" through a series of virtual personae, we shall see evidence of fundamental shifts in the way we create and experience human identity. But it is on the Internet that confrontations with technology as it collides with the sense of human identity are fresh, even raw. In the real-time communities of cyberspace, we are dwellers on the threshold between the real and the virtual, unsure of our footing, inventing ourselves as we go along.

This quotation refers to an outmoded idea of "the way we create and experience human identity". But no definition of self or identity, as we are supposed to understand them traditionally, is provided. The construct being challenged is the assumption that there is a commonly accepted idea of self as a unitary phenomenon. However, this is by no means a prevailing view of identity. Social interaction theorists have presented concepts of identity as a product of group membership, distinctions between social groups, or class and caste, to give only the briefest of references. Among the most subtly developed of these is the notion of self-presentation outlined by Goffman in which interactants collaborate to facilitate the respective images of self that each party tacitly attempts to project. Goffman calls this "face": not "self" but self-presentation. His theory is premised not on an elusive definition of selfhood per se, but on the image of self that social participants put forth as viable means of negotiating normal social life. Managing the boundaries of varying presentations of self is part of this work.

Also included in the history of theoretical writings that discuss identity as an artifact of social context are Simmel, Mead, Schutz, Berger and Luckmann. All view selfhood as a product and process of social forces, whether in the context of everyday interaction, negotiations over meaning and manners, or struggles for social dominance.

In short, in the social sciences, there are notions of self or identity that mostly involve a definition of the individual in relationship to others, not pinned down to a singular presentation but occurring as an artifact of dyads, settings and groups. The aforementioned authors on social identity share an emphasis on negotiation and coconstruction as central to any definition of identity or self. In contrast, postmodern writers on Internet adopt the constructs of Foucault, Jameson and Lacan, alleging that the self is a series of unrelated episodes and connected to society only as a form of limitation and political domination.

The idea of self as varied is not new but a feature of mainstream social theory and take issue with idea that the self is discontinuous and a creation of the individual, under the control of that individual or else conversely controlled as a political unit. These latter premises are essential to the notion that selfhood can be changed in nature by moving to an allegedly anonymous electronic medium.

Self as Being

If we return to the philosophical presuppositions of the notion of the dispersed self, we find the postmodernist argument in still deeper trouble. From the earlier phenomenology of Heidegger we have a less apparently graspable concept than that of the self—but for that reason probably more robust—to wit, Being. Being defies both definition and interpretation by beings themselves, because of its inevitably prior or "already-always" condition of being "thrown" or a product of its history and surrounding practices. Not only that, but because of the inherent elusiveness of a self-definition for Being, beings tend to focus all the more on constructed coherence, as opposed to attempting to evade it. Dreyfus' explanation of basic premises of this phenomenology includes the following arguments:

> Hermeneutic phenomenology, then, is an interpretation of human beings as essentially self-interpreting...We have already seen that our understanding of our being is never fully accessible since 1) it is embodied in skills and 2) we dwell in our understanding like fish in water...3) Our understanding of being is distorted. Since everyday Dasein (Being) does not want to face up to its own interpretive activity and the consequent unsettledness of human being, it uses its everyday understanding to conceal the truth about itself.

> ...Not only is human being interpretation all the way down...but this condition is one of such radical rootlessness that everyone feels fundamentally unsettled (unheimlich), that is, senses that human beings can never be at home in the world. This...is why we plunge into trying to make ourselves at home and secure. Thus the conformist, everyday activities in which human beings seek to give their lives some stable meaning reveal to Heidegger a flight motivated by the preontological understanding each human being has of his or her ultimate ungroundedness.

This is an inverse argument to the one posited in postmodern discussions of Internet: that Internet provides people the opportunity to do what they have always wanted, which is to abandon the confines of a limiting self. For instance, Stone lays out the self as a politically constructed and locatable entity which is thereby open to social control.

> The individual societal actor becomes fixed in respect to geographical coordinates that determine physical locus...by a metaphysics of presence I mean that a (living) body implies the presence within the body of a socially articulated self that is the true site of agency. It is this coupling, rather than the presence of the body alone, that privileges the body as the site of political authentication....Tactics of discipline and control are meant to manage the coupled self with which agency and consequent political authenticity have been constructed to reside.

Stone argues that the more removed the self is from this locatable socially articulated self, the more freedom is available to generate interpretations that suit the participant.

The effect of narrowing bandwidth is to engage more of the participants' interpretive faculties....For symbolic exchange originating at and relating to the surface of the body, narrowing bandwidth has startling effects....Frequently in narrow-bandwidth communication the interpretive faculties of one participant or another are powerfully, even obsessively, engaged.

Another leading post-modern commentator, Poster, likewise claims that in cyberspace, "the self is decentered, dispersed, and multiplied in continuous instability."

Negotiated Order

By contrast we assert, as the ethnomethodological literature illustrates in painstaking detail, that people are engaged in a constant effort to structure experience together and to establish order in conventions of discourse so that shared meanings are possible

The background to this effort is the postulate quoted above from Dreyfus, that coconstructed order is all we have. This is accomplished not only by tacitly establishing agreement on what is presupposed and taken for granted in discourse and social action, but also by the routines of how everyday action and discourse are carried out. The specific situations of discourse are frameworks that cast the context from which interpretations and shareable meaning are generated. The same fundamental practices would apply to text-based discourses, whether anonymous or not: participants cooperate tacitly in setting up a discourse context in which their dialogue is mutually meaningful, and actively manage and coconstruct the orderliness of this dialogue in process. They coordinate a sense of appropriateness and membership from which the sense of "self" is derived.

Linde discusses this process of order building as an individual process as well. Using accounts of life histories, she argues that creating the coherence of a life story is an ongoing effort to reinterpret past events in terms of their relationship to current outcomes. The constructive effort is to form a socially coherent account of the sequence of the otherwise discontinuous events in a life as a unified narrative with logical transitions.

Thus we have to call in question the idea that fragmentation of self would ever be the basis for cultural change. From an ontological perspective experience can be seen as already fragmented, with the work of culture being to organize meanings which are available to individuals as the background for the coconstruction of order. Whether or not there is a separate and dominating political order imposed from "above," the daily construction of order as a fundamental social process has been very well argued and illustrated.

Programming a Self

However, because context is prior to orderly discourse, new contexts do change the means by which order is constructed, and can occasion confusion. There is indeed a socially defined difference between the presentations of "self" that can occur on Internet if people choose to abandon their everyday attributes and the presentations of self that occur within the boundaries of embodied life. It is also true that it is possible to create a "persona" on Internet and for this option to extend to people otherwise unlikely to dissimulate in the physical world. But what does this behavior mean for society at large? While subgroups carry out fantasy lives as Star Trek characters or cross-dressers in the physical social world, they tend to remain marginalized. The premise is that because Internet is more anonymous, even supposedly totally anonymous, more people will take the option to participate in these marginalized roles. This presumes a primacy of fantasy over practical motivations in large numbers of people.

There are many ways in which it appears that Internet culture retains a sensitivity to mainstream motivations, including status indicators, which rightly or wrongly are part of our social sorting mechanisms. Indeed because cues are less available, more is made of less information, according to Correll's study of an electronic cafe. Similarly Wall makes the claim that people respond to e-mail messages in certain domains in part because of small indications of status they may convey: "I have learned the hard way that my .edu address carries more weight than my aol.com address. Having an aol address is akin to living on the wrong side of the tracks."

The content and style of text also convey messages about the writer's background, assumptions, education and orientations. It is difficult if not impossible to create speech or text that is free of these embedded tacit messages, by the very nature of language. Dissimulators learn to manage the tacit messages as well as the explicit ones, but very few have the skill to completely control all levels of the messages they convey. With good reason, we tend not to trust these people.

It may be interesting to contemplate removing all conventional social distinctions, including those between the very wide range of "mainstream" behaviors and all other behavior. The problem is that the historically situated physical person must in fact cope with the implications of these choices, and must act from a "situation". The locus for the integration of experience is not just the politically defined agency of self Stone refers to but rather the historically bounded Being.

In arguments against work in AI that attempts to take context into account, Dreyfus makes comments which are applicable to our case. The central thesis of both AI and the concept of a virtual self is that there are aspects of intelligence and experience that are separable from embodiment by being recreatable in virtuality, that is, out of context. They thus supposedly acquire autonomous existence as independent analytical processes in the one case and independent self-extensions in the other.

While the authors of works describing cyberlife as independent of stuff ally themselves with postmodern philosophy, in the end their arguments appear mechanical and deterministic. They rely on the notion that technology causes and can lead to the existence of something that acts autonomously, whether an artificial mind or an artificial self. Dreyfus' argument in refuting the premise of artificial intelligence is that computers lack "thrownness" into an already existing context of culture and therefore lack the presuppositions required to call out some features as relevant and others as not, that is, lack the ability to form meanings. In a critique of even the relatively humanistic forms of AI research, Dreyfus elaborates arguments against the possibility of programming a context that serve also as arguments against the concept of constructing new selves in cyberspace.

> To be consistent, [AI] would have to treat each type of situation the computer could be in as an object with its prototypical description; then in recognizing a specific situation, the situation or context in which that situation was encountered would determine which foci, goals, etc. were relevant. But where would such a regress stop? Human beings, of course, don't have this problem. They are, as Heidegger puts it, already in a situation, which they constantly revise....[A program] is not always-already-in-a-situation. Even if it represents all possible types of human situations, it represents them from the outside like a Martian or a god. It isn't situated in any of them, and it may be impossible to program it to behave as if it were....All these uniquely human capacities provide a "richness" or a "thickness" to our way of being-in-the-world and thus seem to play an essential role in situatedness, which in turn underlies all intelligent behavior.

By the same logic that argues context can't be programmed, we would assert the context-creation claimed on behalf of MUD players is not really a context. The MUD situations described by Turkle and Stone, of elaborately specified scenarios of rooms, furniture, food, creatures, vistas, personal appearances, gender, ritual, relationships to create a social environment, in light of the above resemble the attempt of the artificial intelligence programmer to recreate contexts in order to be able to make sense of human language. What this specified life lacks is the grounding in Being that pre-establishes situatedness for real life experience. Throughout Dreyfus' work on Heidegger this grounding is categorically asserted to come from the body and the conditions of embodiment.

To the extent that there is an attempt to "create" selves distinct from a historical embodied self, these selves are more like programs than they are identities. Turkle argues that this boundary is precisely the point.

> In the daily practice of many computer users, windows have become a powerful metaphor for thinking about the self as a multiple, distributed system. The self is no longer playing different roles in different settings at different times....The life practice of windows is that of a decentered self that exists in many worlds and plays many roles at the same time.......As more people spend more time in these virtual spaces, some go so far as to challenge the idea of giving any priority to RL [Real Life] at all. 'After all, says one dedicated MUD player and IRC user, 'why grant such superior status to the self that has the body when the selves that don't have bodies are able to have different kinds of experiences?'

But, how can we call them selves if they lack the situated intelligence of historical embodiment? They exist as artifacts of that being that types them in. Therefore they cannot be claimed to have equality, since the being can easily continue without these "selves".

They, on the other hand, will discontinue without the basis of the person in the body, since as programs, they lack the situated intelligence to even pretend to be "someone".

Thus this argument of independent multiple selves depends upon a notion that being and its generative context could be specified. This appears to be an unsubstantiated notion of self. The extension of this to a subsequent change of culture is even thinner.

Internet Requires Boundary Shifts

Another way to cast the fragmentation that is claimed for Internet activity is to view Internet as a new social domain where boundaries that pertain to the physical world or prior domains of convention have not yet been worked out. This gives rise to the "ludic" quality eloquently described by Stone, simply because of the disorientation occasioned by ambiguity in our conventional sense of where boundaries between contrasting domains of experience should be drawn. The primacy of the "thrown" context would be an argument for the dramatic effects that occur when our expected distinctions fail to apply.

This can happen easily with new technology, because so much of our ordering of the world is tied to artifacts and minute processes, that is, appears as an integrated whole that includes physical and linguistic dimensions. New media occasion shifts in boundaries. One illustrative case is Orlikowski's account of how a groupware program for technical service support, by textualizing service conversations, makes knowledge differentials in a workgroup more visible, occasioning negotiations over the institutional effect of the tacit processes thus made available for view.

Studies of technological impact would not be taken up if it weren't presumed that this different mode of communicative action somehow changes what is said, how it is said, to whom it is said, and what its effect is, within a wide range of social domains. We do expect that the way communication is divided up, directed, received and interpreted is affected by electronic media: the universal availability of broadcast text, asynchronous dialogue, and real-time transmission being three major threshold effectors to be found in the medium.

These can be explained using the less radical construct of shifting boundaries for preexisting conventions. There are many ways to look at boundary issues. Three boundaries bear on the present topic: social/technical boundary; real/virtual boundary, and public/private boundary. All of these are embedded in the arguments about the postmodernism of Internet.

Social/technical boundary

Before we accept the premise that technology changes things, we need to consider technology itself as a social construct, whose definition as an artifact is prior to any social effect it can be presumed to have, since it is a social effect itself. The argument posed in all of the cyberspace literature—that electronic media change culture—is patently circular in the light of the socially situated existence and use of any technology. This point has been discussed by Bloomfield and Vurdubakis.

> Our argument...is that any account that takes the "properties" of a particular technology as its starting point, is from the beginning caught up in those practices that generate and sustain the objectively given quality of those properties. Hence this type of account will, however reluctantly, tend to reinforce the whole notion of a technology as something that develops outside, as it were, the social relations on which it impacts.

This is a different point from the seemingly related theme in Life on the screen, that:

> Just as musical instruments can be extensions of the mind's construction of sound, computers can be extensions of the mind's construction of thought. ...The computer can be...experienced as an object on the border between self and not-self. Or, in a new variant on the story of Narcissus, people are able to fall in love with the artificial worlds they have created or that have been built for them by others. People are able to see themselves in the computer. The machine can seem a second self...

Both quotations talk about technology as a constructed "object" in some way. But Bloomfield and Vurdubakis emphasize the priority of social construction and social understanding, while Turkle refers to the individual construction and extension of self as an artifact of technology. This is a critical distinction.

The difference in implication—between sharing an understanding of a socially constructed object and creating an extension of the individual self—is the difference between participating in common understandings and the presumption that definition of self and object emerge singly from individual minds.

Further implied is that they do so because of features of external artifacts. In the latter case, shared conventions do not apply. In the former they do. If the social construction of "what technology is" and how it is bounded off from the social, are prior ontological events, then the so-called individual projections about technology must be artifacts of that social construction, not of the subsequently defined element labeled technology.

Real/Virtual Boundary

Another boundary issue is the one posited between "real" and "virtual." This is a strange boundary to come up in the postmodernist context, because presumably such a boundary does not exist in the underlying philosophy of constructivism. Yet both Stone and Turkle, while asserting that this boundary has been dissolved, continually revert to the premise of that boundary as a backdrop for discussion.

> The war of desire and technology is about science fiction, in the sense that it is about emergent technologies, shifting boundaries between the living and the non-living, optional embodiment...in other words, about the everyday world as a cyborg habitat....I am interested in prosthetic communication for what it shows of the "real" world that might otherwise go unnoticed. And I am interested because of the potential of cyberspace for emergent behavior, for new social forms that arise in a circumstance in which body, meet, place, and even space mean something quite different from our accustomed understanding.

Taken to its logical conclusion, Turkle writes, the ultimate result is a disappearance of conventional reality (whatever that might be) from the world outside the computer into the virtual world expressed within the computer. "As the boundaries erode between real and the virtual, the animate and inanimate, the unitary and the multiple self, the question becomes: Are we living life on the screen or in the screen?".

Here it is assumed that there has been an agreed upon "reality" in the past but that we are headed toward something virtual and that a life in text has the ability to compete with the life experienced by the rest of the body. This existence requires a great deal of sitting and typing, which the body ought to object to and the senses should find deprivational. It expresses what Turkle herself has more plausibly described in her prior book The second self as disembodiment in the hacker subculture. But it is by no means clear why this apparent dysfunctionality should take over as the locus for life that formerly happened outside the screen.

There are certainly ways in which virtualness overcomes past structures of accountability, as for example, sensational cases in the financial markets in which brokers become caught up in the manipulation of very large numbers in a very short time and lose billions of dollars, acting as if in a game when in fact they are dealing with people's life savings (L. Introna, personal communication). This distancing from accountability could be attributed to the complexity and speed of the transactions and the youth of those manipulating the programs, both of which are associated with a radically different technology of trading. It may be "only money," but these effects do something to the physical circumstances of the people whose money has become a virtual game to the trader.

However, if we are going to depend on phenomenological arguments, we have to consider that at least in significance, everything exists by agreement. Thus this past reality set up by postmodern authors is a straw creation in the argument about virtuality of Internet. Or, conversely, Internet only appears to be virtual, assuming there is a distinction, and has as substantial a reality as any physical object or "hard" social convention, like money.

Pubic/private boundary

Another key boundary for the discussion is the public-private distinction as revealed in Internet self-presentations. This boundary must be renegotiated both in on-line text-based discourse and in the "advertisement for oneself" represented by the graphics-based home page with links to a network of topics the host feels comprise his on-line surroundings. Speaking to the public/private distinction, postmodernists argue that Internet is essentially a private domain, an extension of the individual's mind and attributes—in fact so private and anonymous that social identity no longer is bounded by physical existence attributes.

We view Internet as public. But its illusion of privacy presents a boundary problem. This view has been discussed in various contexts. For new users or users of entirely recreational domains, this illusion may obtain. In Internet contexts based in conventional purposes like professional discussion lists, the effort to find satisfactory boundaries between personal and private may be awkward at times, with inadvertent transgressions being both public and recorded. But list conventions and those of other on-line groups that reflect embodied groups, are closely tied to the conventions of the same participants in face-to-face professional meetings.

In a new medium, new behaviors are ventured, exploiting features of the electronic context. Boundaries are discovered and new coherent forms of social organization then become established as appropriate behavior for a domain. The issues become resolved within specific conversational and professional contexts, then arise again as new technologies create new contexts and forms of use. The key point is that they do become resolved and that this resolution occurs by means of social action within the domain, whether through guidelines imposed by a list owner, sanctions expressed by other members, or simply the professional socialization and motivations that guide people to use Internet in the first place.

The role of anonymity in the fragmented self

These boundary issues come up as part of the assumptions embedded in the notion that Internet lends itself to a diffracted identity: if the technical world is separate, if Internet is "virtual," whether Internet is private or public—all of these premises greatly affect the notion that on-line communications are a projection of the liberated imagination without real-world consequences.

> Frederic Jameson wrote that in a postmodern world, the subject is not alienated but fragmented. He explained that the notion of alienation presumes a centralized, unitary self who could become lost to himself or herself. But if, as a postmodernist sees it, the self is decentered and multiple, the concept of alienation breaks down. All that is left is an anxiety of identity.

The key to this diffracted identity is anonymity. The decentered quality is seen as an artifact of the separation of expressions from the physical person. "The body in question sits at a computer terminal somewhere, but the locus of sociality that would in an older dispensation be associated with this body goes on in a space which is quite irrelevant to it."

> In contrast with the relentlessly monistic articulations of physical and virtual space that law and science favor, let us juxtapose the mode of the technosocial, of reinvention and encounter in a technological space viewed as itself a social and physical environment, as a kind of nature. In the idealized view of such a space, the very elements that Foucault saw as being suppressed in the process of "gridding" reassert themselves in novel ways—irruptively constituting identities that are simultaneously technological and social, a catastrophic emergence of the ludic and unpredictable at the very heart of the ordered mathematical structures that by their very nature seek to suppress it. This process is possible, in fact inevitable, because the technosocial, the social mode of the computer nets, evokes unruly multiplicity as an integral part of social identity.

The "technosocial" realm which "irruptively constitutes identities that are simultaneously technological and social" depends on a separation of body from the view of others with whom one interacts: the technical is the mediator between that physical person and others. The means by which the ensuing multiplicity is achieved then is anonymity, unlocatability.

The evidence for the view outlined above is selected from users talking about their relationships in multi-user domains (muds) or from dialogues carried out over muds. This population does illustrate, at least for a while, certain features of the argument. However, Turkle shows that many users abandon muds, seeing them post hoc as "useless and addictive." Stone's book covers the story of a male psychotherapist who posed as a disabled woman advising other women on intimate aspects of their lives.

The telling point is the subsequent outrage when his accurate social descriptors are discovered.

In all of the stories new kinds of interactions do became available for the actors, but the substantive outcomes often tend to be either nonproductive, or counterproductive outrage over the poses and the disclosures that result from false representation. The anonymity by which the "selves" are achieved in the end seems to be the obstacle to any results that we count as "real" or satisfying. Besides, anonymity itself is virtual.

Counter-examples to the Postmodern argument

The philosophical and sociological weaknesses of the postmodern position for Internet as a liberation from physical identity. Relying primarily on Dreyfus' interpretations of Heidegger's phenomenology, we have pointed out that, opposite to seeking liberation from the constrictions of social identity, it is more likely from this perspective that in the absence of self-existent meaning, people desperately seek to create form out of chaos. Their social conventions, behaviors, and self-descriptions are directed to that end. We have also pointed out the lack of an agreed-on definition of identity of the kind that both Stone and Turkle assume to be a general understanding, that is, one person, one identity.

Finally, we have sketched out the kinds of boundary issues that the case for fragmented identity tacitly depends on: a social/technical boundary, a real/virtual boundary, and a public/private boundary. By laying out these broad premises, containing within them unstated assumptions, the postmodern authors cited lay themselves open to dispute by counterexample. We will take advantage of this opportunity to provide counterpoints to the material on fragmentation by showing a variety of ways in which the theory does not work.

Two of the main underpinning premises of a radically different cyberculture are virtuality and anonymity. We will discuss both of them briefly. Virtuality implies that Internet is a "space" that is self-existent, not relying upon institutions, commercial interests, or conventions. Because this "space" allows for electronic exchanges that happen so quickly they resemble real-time interactions; it gives rise to the appearance of being a world unto itself, totally different from the everyday world. Since it is possible, at least by agreement and temporarily, to block identification of interactants in this space, virtuality allows the illusion of anonymity.

Anonymity is the fundamental basis of the notion of multiple identities operating freely in cyberspace. A particular text persona can be separated from another one. These two or more presumably never have to "cross paths," that is, experience the consequences of contradictions that would apply to a consistent physical person who can be proved to be the one who carried out certain acts or spoke certain words. Therefore it is reasoned that the various personae are now free from social boundaries and hence from accountability for each others' constraints. Stone devotes a considerable amount of space to this concept in her section on multiple personalities. But courts of law exist for the very purpose of making the links between actions, words, and specific individuals. This is because even in the nonvirtual world, there is a constant inconsistency among the sides of an individual that are presented in varying contexts. This is what "evidence" is all about. In cyberspace it is possible to cover one's tracks somewhat more easily than in the everyday world, and therefore to make unaccountability more plausible.

But anonymity depends upon virtuality, and virtuality is in fact just another construct. Internet may have an emergent property of giving rise to certain capabilities and behaviors, but these exist by agreement just like everything else in the social world. Internet is a large collection of machines with communications capabilities between them, owned and supported by real institutions and real dollars. The concepts of virtuality and anonymity both depend upon forgetting these facts.

First will examine how anonymous Internet is, then how virtual it is. We will look at the political premise underlying the idea of "freedom" on Internet. We will use secondary research that suggests experimentally that Internet is less effective used alone and anonymously than it is when supplemented with other modes of communication, if the user wants to accomplish something as simple as solving an experimental problem with an Internet-based team. We will see what happens when someone tries out a "persona" on a professional discussion list and thus crosses the personal/professional boundary.

Finally, will examine a selection of home pages for ideas on how they differ from interactive text communications. Home page creators would rather build context for a diverse but unified identity than work in separate and unconnected domains. The linking capability of home pages provides their owners with some unique ways to build social context around themselves and present it to random viewers more effectively than their own filtered accounts about themselves would do. In this way personal home pages show less anonymity and more social embeddedness, and in many cases more integration of facets, than everyday life does.

Internet is the Panopticon

The constructivist description of Internet as a playground for the unbounded self fails to take into account the flip side of Foucault's arguments as they especially apply on Internet: the premise of the Panopticon or constant view of individuals through parasocietal mechanisms that influence behavior simply because of the possibility of being observed. Although Internet dialogue may provide a degree of privacy in the moment, it eliminates the ultimate privacy of all communications carried out over it. Persons play at multiplicity at their indefinite peril, experiencing and experimenting with more freedom from social constraints, and at the same time letting down the guards of normal social and political caution that generations of historical context have imbued. The following is a private reflection upon this possibility, posted to an Internet news group.

> . . . what about Usenet or personal home pages? It's now possible for anybody to publish anything about anybody else...With a search engine like DejaNews it's possible to trace back all old postings from somebody...Besides postings to usenet people also leave info by signing guest books on web pages etc...The digital technology makes everybody sort of transparent because you can combine all different

> data on somebody...I can't undo everything I did on the net the last couple of years, but my future employer will be able to read most of it ...It seems that some people's dogma, 'Our lives will inevitably become visible to others, so the real issue is mutual visibility, achieving a balance of power by enabling us to watch the people who are watching us,' already became true. I don't have a problem really with the fact that all about me becomes visible to others. It's just that I'd rather not see *all* available to *everybody*... Even so-called anonymous remailers are no guarantee of anonymity as their records can always be turned over to the authorities.

Despite the availability of encryption mechanisms, the fact is that users of Internet who are not protecting specifically sensitive information like money transfers, medical records, or company financial information, do not encrypt their activities. Although access is practically free, protection is not. Below is a description of only the latest of many items of concern relating to privacy.

> In a new twist related to privacy problems, one of the more major Web search services, the "Magellan Internet Guide" from the McKinley Group, Inc., has implemented a feature which allows anyone to "spy" on other people's searches. Called the "Search Voyeur", the mechanism automatically shows the text of 20 current, randomly selected searches, refreshed every 20 seconds.

They certainly haven't been trying to hide it; it was prominently mentioned in one of their press releases....Even a brief viewing of the searches flying by suggests a substantial privacy risk. Search keywords often include individuals' names associated with various actions or activities. While some of the searches can best be described as "amusing", it doesn't take too long to see others that are troubling at best and potentially significant privacy violations at worst.

No "Original" Means Permanent Record: Internet and Political Context.

Following through on the implications of the virtuality and "no original" nature of Internet communications outlined by Turkle as features of postmodernism, then, in contrast to incriminating paper documents, Internet communications do indeed have no "original". This means they can neither be fetched back nor shredded. They cannot be counted. There is no possibility of a Watergate break-in to retrieve regrettable posts. There is no guarantee of control over one's creations once they have been let loose. Since the earliest days of e-mail, posts could be re-posted or broadcast. Now search engines mean that posts not only go where they might, but also can be traced wherever they have gone.

The same postmodern theory that frames the "no original" concept also asserts that the "meaning" of these objects is applied post hoc, by the reader of the text. There thus is a multiplicity of possible meanings and interpretations for a communication that has been let loose on the Net. In the context of a semipermanent existence, powerful search engines, and diffuse storage, the downstream impact of future interpretations is more a dread than a liberation from binding social conditions of age, gender, race, and class (not to mention religious and political affiliation). While default social meanings are removed, others may be added according to the biases of the reader.

In addition to the direct ways that people leave traces of themselves, there are indirect ways that data can be collected. Most web-sites have the capability to collect some information about visitors. Employers and service providers can collect data about individuals who use their networks to connect to the Internet or send and receive e-mail. In sum, the anonymity projected by Gumpert and others to Internet transactions is far from real. Internet users face prospects of micro-observation, and the data collected thereby have no finite end to their existence or availability to inspection at a later time. Thus virtual anonymity presents an illusion of privacy and a trap of almost unlimited potential by inducing people to cross critical public/private boundaries.

First Amendment rights are a major policy backdrop to the freedom experienced in Internet communications in democratic countries. But these are subject to constant political struggle. News items concerning suppression or control of Internet use in China, Singapore, Burma and Iran support this. Both Iran and Burma have sought to control sites and their contents; CompuServe threatened to remove an administrative center in Germany because of government restrictions on Nazi writing and images.

The point is that anonymity is preserved by agreement only. It is possible for any net-savvy person to trace an individual, and the Internet service provider (ISP) has a record of the account-holder. As well, there are many openly hostile entities involved in Internet observation, if not here, then in the wider world that has become part of the electronic community.

Cyberspace Depends on Real Machines in Real Geography. Virtual identity depends heavily upon the very real physical infrastructure of Internet. It may be true that Internet has no "center" and constitutes a form of self-organizing system when its circuits are in order. According to one of Turkle's subjects: "It's like a brain, self-organizing, nobody controlling it, just growing up out of the connections that an infant makes...It's a new kind of organism...No way you could have built it by planning it."

However, it is clear that Internet is supported by large-scale institutions and infrastructure, starting with its history in the Defense Advance Research Project Agency (darpa). A news item about network failure throughout the state of Minnesota points to the still close correspondence between our existing institutional structures and the structures that constitute Internet segments.

The primary network that serves Minnesota (the Minnesota Regional Network) was cut off from the Internet for 12 hours today [September 15, 1996]. (My understanding is that *all* major nets and systems, private and public, in Minnesota ultimately get their connection to the rest of the world through MR Net. PGN.)

Other outages, at Stanford and America Online, also reported on risks and elsewhere, underscore the dependence of the virtual world on physical objects and connections that are specifically located in space and affect geographical areas when they malfunction, causing a breakdown in the illusion of alocality. We tend to think of Internet as structured according to provider domains, but who thinks of the State of Minnesota as a relevant Internet boundary?

In short, the transparency of the medium leads to a presumption that Internet is not only less socially determined than it really is, but also that Internet is less geographically bounded than it really is. It is true that global communications can occur in what appears to be real-time when things are working. But the infrastructure that provides that geographic transparency is in rl located at some place.

Within the context of a professional list in which people go by their own names, a new participant acts as enthusiastic discoverer of a list-relevant product, when he is in fact a part of the organization that sells the product. The list tolerates the occasional promotion of relevant bpr services and process model software and more frequently discusses the merits of various methods, products and providers.

Sometimes providers or enthusiastic users will join those discussions, but always in the capacity of "themselves." However, their institutional connection is a highly relevant fact about that self. The fact that someone is a principal at a major consulting firm, for instance, becomes an obvious context for any comments he/she will make about the organization's products or services.

On lists that combine buyers and sellers of services in general discussion, there is a notable constraint for bona fide members not obviously to be selling, since that removes them from the conversational context and places them in another, less effective mode of participation, "advertising", which lessens their credibility for the discussion context.

At the same time, no reasonable person expects them to debunk their own employer's offerings. Therefore an appropriate degree of promotion pared down to the relevance conventions of the general open discussion is accepted and expected.

This is itself an identifiable mode and convention of communication on such a list. It allows people to participate authentically and yet remain within the bounds of professional obligations imposed by speaking in public with the employer's logo, sign-off, or .com address being obvious to all readers. As in formal meetings, participants are speaking for themselves but with the awareness that they should not speak against their employer's interest. Thus the effective management of social boundaries within a context that mixes both institutional and personal statuses is a critical skill for effective participation in the list. Indeed, not observing the fact that there is a boundary problem and trying to isolate the context down to one of the two domains implied for all of the participants becomes a violation.

Boundary maintenance and cohesion are key skills of the electronic domain precisely because normal constraints do not apply. An effective member of this group, which has no formal admission requirements, is someone with a legitimate and at least partially informed interest in the topic of bpr, whether employed by an organization or self-employed, student or academic. And participants should have the capacity to "be themselves" in order that their contributions be construed as their own authentic thoughts, not just public relations for the institution or business agenda in the background. To overemphasize the personal is to be irrelevant to the discussion; to overemphasize the institutional is to lose credibility by turning into an advertiser. This is boundary issue number one.

Anonymity is Part of the Magic, but Not of the Effectiveness. Boundary issue number two is the boundary between the list, an electronic medium, and other ways to realize the relationships that may develop. The first step away from list behavior is one-to-one e-mail exchanges. In these exchanges, people may affirm their support for or disagreement with the positions of others in more personal ways than they care to broadcast, expand on secondary interests, and get to know each other. These more elaborated messages cross a tacit public/private boundary, which is why they are taken to the "side channel." These communications may result in longer term electronic acquaintance that can sustain a hiatus yet retain interest. The next step in boundary crossing is to change communication genres. Thus some one-on-one e-mail exchanges may move to telephone conversations. And in the final case, of course, personal meetings occur either deliberately or by chance. Members of lists are often members of the same professional groups. Physical meeting is always a possibility, and this possibility tends to be increased by electronic meeting

Correll's study of this topic shows that in many groups there appears to be a drive toward making in-person contact with people interacted with on-line. Katz and Aspden also have data indicating that a large number of friendships are newly established in virtual space among people who did not know each other before, and that a substantial minority of these acquaintanceships gravitate to face-to-face meetings. So, anonymity is desirable perhaps for some portion of the Internet population, but there is no reason to think that this represents a cultural change, since there is ample evidence that another possibly larger portion of the population of users take their Internet opportunities to other domains when they appear promising.

An interesting study by Myers addresses this second boundary issue empirically, and handily supports our argument. Myers' study was carried out in Austin, Texas, with the establishment of a bulletin board, originally using aliases. His analysis breaks out system expert leadership from social expert leadership, the latter being those most skilled at starting and mediating discussions, including new members, and generally taking ownership for the quality and inclusiveness of the dialogue. Myers' experiment then went on to a second stage in which groups appointed by him were instructed collectively and competitively to solve problems.

At that time it was proposed that aliases be dropped and real names be used. An interesting finding was that people classified by Myers as "system experts" preferred real names while "social experts tended to prefer aliases. Some people thus did maintain aliases in the second exercise. The paper discusses the rationales for aliases, a clue to which is given in the title "Anonymity is part of the magic."

Producing Outcomes Requires Media Flexibility. What interests us here is the fact that in the problem-solving exercise, the group of system experts went outside the electronic boundary to collaborate and resorted to telephone communications when needed. Their willingness to use real identities, including demographic information such as place of employment, location, and telephone number, in harmony with the boundary-crossing strategy, enabled them to perform better on the problem-solving goal, whereas the alias users continued to use only electronic media.

Social experts found their skills poorly suited to accomplishing the task-oriented game goals and either refused to (or could not) adopt alternative on-line strategies....Perhaps the most significant result of the game play was the use of alternative media (telephone, face-to-face contact) by the system expert leaders to quickly relay information among team members and thereby gain an advantage in game play. Those participants more skilled in social context manipulation played by implicit game rules...and communicated with each other solely through [the bulletin board].

This finding is significant and pertinent to our thesis. It is supported indirectly by other studies of media choice involving electronic communications as one among many possibilities in suggesting that social activity grounded in a task or purpose employs multiple media (whatever is appropriate) for accomplishing the purpose. It is also supported by genre research. And it fits into a general thesis in sociolinguistic research indicating that each style in a linguistic repertoire is used seamlessly in an overall communication and social action strategy, the choice of medium has meaning and effect, and that any grounded purpose will be the guiding formative context for selection of media (or language strategy), even if one medium is preferred .

The finding that the social context manipulators preferred aliases and in some cases would not play without them suggests a contradiction between the working expression of self and the "play" one, whether or not the separation is needed. We would have to say these participants were not good integrators. Their reliance on a single medium, the electronic one, also shows a highly specific purpose: that of communicating electronically as an end in itself or as a separation of the electronic purpose from purposes in general.

The implications of Myers' study then are that the presentation multipliers or dissimulators may exist as a population, but their purposes do not exist outside of the virtual medium. This is a limited legitimation of the claims for a "virtual world." On the other hand, equally frequent and proficient users of electronic media tend not only to integrate their "working" person with their electronic one but to have goals that are socially embedded and have a wider context for action than simply the electronic one, even if the purpose in question is an electronic game. Not only is the context for action wider in the sense that it extends into an embodied world with consequences and possibilities that have material substance, but the means employed to achieve these extend beyond the electronic boundary. The electronic medium then becomes one means of many, whether or not it is the dominant means.

The real difficulty Internet users face is the effect in the real world of boundary ambiguities in the virtual one. In daily life, as well as in any institutionalized form of communication, e.g. business letters, publications, there is a known intended audience for the presentation; and there are tacit ground rules for the conduct of communication in the medium.

The Personal Home Page as Presentation of an Integrated Self

We have addressed above the distinction between public and private domains: how these domains become transformed or shift their boundaries in group behavior.

Similar but distinct issues arise in personal home pages. The personal home page is a recent phenomenon of as yet unexplored impact. The effectiveness of commercial home pages as a medium for business is still a topic in debate. The commercial home page contrasts with the personal home page as a novel medium because although its methods are different, its contents tend to be predictable as commercially formatted and presented information geared to an audience and intended to sell to that audience.

There is an interesting discussion of how commercial Web sites need to become more communitarian in nature in order to reap a benefit. So there are social theory issues to be explored even with regard to these sites. But they do not yet exhibit as openly the experimentation with self-presentation that personal sites do. Their ultimate purpose is well understood rather than being emergent, although their means may still provide some surprises. Commercial home pages are clearly public documents and as such form a business genre with their own impact with perhaps more scrutiny and accountability than some printed business publicity.

The ways personal home pages are being constructed as a presentation of self add further evidence for rejecting arguments about fragmentation of the individual in cyberspace. Now numbering in the millions, these are essentially people's self-created windows on themselves and as such are a construction of self offered to the random viewer. Pertinent details of what is important to the host, as well as links to other topics, are typical of home pages. While there are varying implications of home pages, discussed in the following, a key feature is that they move in the opposite direction of what cyperspace postmodernists claim: rather than fragmenting the self, personal home pages are attempts to integrate the individual, make a personal statement of identity, and show in a stable, replicable way what the individual stands for and what is deemed important. This tends to be an inclusive self-presentation that is less selective than individual media someone might employ for a purpose. It is curriculum vitae, personal advertisement, reflective medium, and art all rolled into one presentation. In this way it is more integrative than conventional media.

Ambiguity of Public/Private Boundary: Who Is the Audience? We said earlier that each new medium seems to require new boundary adjustments. One of the interesting features of pages we selected is the ambiguity of social boundaries encountered there. Some home page creators appear to perceive a more private world of readers than is in fact the case. Frequently the pages are not so much personally private but are located at an intermediate level of privacy, the sheltered environment of a peer group or work group. The problem is that anyone can access these pages. That is a fact of their existence. Yet how much social understanding do the creators of pages have, and how accordingly do they mediate their self-expression to account for the possibilities of a limitless audience?

The audience problem is more bounded in the physical world. At any given time and place in physical life, we can look around and see who else is there. Based on an assessment, we adjust our presentation of self. There is a common social expectation that we are supposed to understand the implications and messages conveyed in our public actions and self-expression and that we are in some way at least socially if not legally accountable for their effects.

The vernacular phrase "asking for trouble" conveys this normative view that we are accountable for mediating our relationship to the world in such a way that we minimize negative effects, or that if negative effects occur, we must try to show we are innocent of having provoked them or "asked for" them. All of this is implied in such descriptions of behavior as "circumspect," "proper," "conventional," "normal," or "discreet". These concepts are used routinely in courts of law, which refer frequently to social convention to establish the reasonableness of clients' behavior.

The standards are ambiguous in the virtual medium because there is no physical co-presence. Members of virtual groups may know other members "face-to-face" (F2F) as the contrasting medium is called, before or after the fact, through common employment, profession or interests. However the majority will probably never meet. The home page, non-directional as it is in audience selection, offers even less likelihood of meetings between presenters and browsers than chat rooms or lists because the home page is not based primarily in dialogue and lacks the filters this provides.

The home page viewing is the meeting; and most pages are set up as one-sided personal introductions. By contrast to the random nature of the home page audience, in traditional self-presentation formats, professional, personal or political, the nature and numbers of the audiences are explicit. In home page "advertisements for one's self", audience is a self-selected unknown. There may be a presumption that the home page in and of itself will be an audience definer, but presenters have little knowledge of the range and size of potential audiences. It is thus possible to construct a presentation of self for an imagined audience while the actual audiences vary.

Given that there is no copresence or standard audience information, how is an individual to assess what is proper, circumspect, or normal? These terms imply a social frame of reference based in public/private distinctions and conventions founded on physical copresence and the personal accountability implied in it. In addition to making the presenter cognizant of audience and thus providing the opportunity to mediate the message, whether verbal or visual, copresence enables the presenter to avoid undesired audiences. On the home page there is no turning away, averting the gaze, or changing the subject as a response to unexpected audience changes.

Thus a more explicit choice of information is involved in unilateral presentation of self, because conventions are less well established. While conventions exist for the unilateral presentation of self in the form of the curriculum vitae, resume, biography, head shot, portfolio, bibliography, and so forth, these artifacts all have—and are consciously designed to have—a focus on an objective. The artifact shares a vocabulary of symbols with the designated audience.

The formalisms themselves become artifacts that speak of the presenter. Does the resume have a succinct statement of objectives at the top? Is the information scannable, does the content reflect relevant and current material? All of these supra-artifacts are part of the process of judging the artifact within the context of a specific objective.

Internet Requires Boundary Redefinition. Home page presenters tend to act as if this narrow focus would be a waste of the medium. Precisely because the viewer is not scanning a linear document but selecting topics to pursue, the home page presenter's challenge as a media artist is to exploit this capability by providing more than the flat page. The links allow in-depth views of particular themes, thus providing far more dimensionality than anything that can be achieved on a page.

However, the home page, unlike the Usenet group or discussion list, is unilateral, at least at the outset. Lists depend entirely on dialogue. Home pages can stand alone as presentations. Thus to the extent that they lack intrinsic interactivity they also lack the excitement or "heat" of discourse. Home pages may adopt conventions of interactivity to heighten presentation dynamics, while operating in a unilateral mode. A subtext of many personal home pages is a tacit acknowledgment of the fact that the home page, by lacking interaction, is cool in tone, if we assume warmth to be a function of interactivity and the opportunity to generate feeling and relationship.

The home page seems to bend over backward to pretend to be interactive by being preemptively disclosive about the self. Without the preliminaries of two people "feeling each other out" to sense what would be appropriate to disclose, the home page jumps to state "this is who I am." Who-I-am tends to be expressed in a photograph, a list of interests which are active by being clickable, and a list of friends which is also active. Thus one is invited unilaterally to engage in an exploration that normally would occur at least dyadically. Indeed the dyadic nature of it would be the purpose for finding out about the person in the first place.

Authenticity involves a perception of another person and representation of self that corresponds to an appropriate and appropriately disclosive communication according to conventions of communication for the speech event, the social group, the other visual cues the person is giving off. It is possible to accomplish this, although edited, in e-mail interactions but not in a billboard-style presentation. As the presenters perceive this lack, we suggest they strive to overcome it.

Home pages as a social context

We reviewed many home pages for this chapter and will use a few to illustrate some examples of shifting boundaries in self-presentation and public versus private ambiguity. One home page belongs to "Mary," an attractive working professional single mother with a young son. Mary shows several informal photographs of herself and her son, as well as her workplace, colleagues and interests. A second home page belongs to Tabatha, a noted Web queen. Tabatha's home page has many links, stunning photographs of Tabatha, who is a software professional; and among many interesting subpages, there is Tabatha's "Male Bag" which publishes letters from Web fans of Tabatha's, all men. Tabatha selects choice fan letters for her shawingg logo, meaning that these letters expressed effective praise. Another interesting home page belongs to Ted Ko, who works in a telecommunications research lab and has an "outrageous" but not offensive page, with reference to the "Cuddles" site, a romantic poem apparently written to a girlfriend, sites of his former colleagues at MIT, and other interests.

We have selected these home pages because they are normal successful attractive pages that are interesting and yet illustrate boundary problems. There are certainly many pages we could look at that are bizarre and that lend credence if not to the dissolution of the self, then at least to the notion that cyberspace is a "ludic" frontier. For instance, a page devoted to celebrity deaths might be censored from a corporate-sponsored site (although "death pools" betting on which celebrities will die next, are not), but is put up by someone who works as a clerk at a video store and a janitor at a church (photo of lovely traditional stone church). The professional self of this page host doesn't conflict with his slightly morbid pet topic, although a child pornography interest might. Thus while extending some general social boundaries, the page does not create a serious boundary conflict.

Public/Private or Personal/Professional Boundary. One thing that becomes clear about home pages is that they represent tacit social contexts of the presenters. Presenters will have either physical social contexts of real friends and colleagues, or virtual social contexts of Net friends and topic groups, or both. Boundary issues become clear when presenters change contexts. One home page that appeared particularly contemporary in its freewheeling cheerful self-disclosure, Ted Ko's, seemed out of context at first because it resided on the site of a telecommunications research lab. Telephone companies tend to have retained strong traditional corporate cultures with regard to self-expression, despite widespread changes in the market environments and structures within which they operate.

For instance, the Cuddles site link on Ted's page just touches the boundary between cute affection and too much tickling. Below is a selection of Cuddles material.

These are just examples of Tal attacks. Just enjoy them for what they are... (POUNCE OUT FROM NET ONTO TIM) (POUNCE TIM) (BOUNCE TIM) (FLOUNCE TIM) (TROUNCE TIM) (HUG) (hug) (Bouncy hug) (tickling cuddles) (runs away) (moment of silence) (hear hooves trampling down mountain) (Tal on horse, waving fuzzy sword, Charges Tim) (Tickle Tim with fuzzy sword!!!) (chuckles to self) Well you did ask.... (giggles) (cuddle)Tal Cuddles site from Ted Ko's link

Two interesting features of this are:

1) Ted Ko's use of it on his home page to indicate a "softer" interest of his and a "fun" side of himself. However, it is only a reference to another site, not his own home page information. We can see that this is something that Ted visits, thinks is fun, but in terms of identity, it isn't Ted. It's just a pointer he has provided;

2) The boundary situation of the Cuddles site itself, which is that it is playful, slightly intrusive in an emotional way, yet never transgresses any serious boundaries. It is playful and Òopen" but not exhibitionistic. The very fun of Cuddles is that it is safe and yet intimate.

Ted Ko's links, located on his corporate web site, thus present a context-bending, boundary-confusing situation. Normally the presentation of employees on company media would represent company standards. Yet this home page represents the individual. It could be inconsistent for a high-tech research lab to restrict innocuous content of its brilliant staff's home pages just as it would be inappropriate to tell them how to dress, beyond basic shared conventions of propriety.

We reviewed other home pages in the lab list and found that the rest of them, if they existed at all, conformed more to our expectation of a telco electrical engineering style: personable, and about as disclosing as members would be to a visitor, describing a few tastes, interests, pets, family. The lab director had an especially circumspect page focused on research interests.

Ted may already have begun to affect his co-workers with his own style. For instance an Asian manager in the lab describes liking "hot, spicy food" a disclosure we venture he might have come up with to try to keep up with the kicky style of his young colleague Ted. His presentation is more disclosing than it might previously have been in talking about his personal likes, but hardly gives away any truly personal information. Ted, on the other hand, remains within the realm of propriety while disclosing quite a bit.

Distributed Contexts. To explain Ted's difference from his immediate environment, we looked for another social context for his page. This was easily discovered by tracing back to his recent alma mater, mit, and the home pages of his friends and colleagues there. Suddenly the normalcy, indeed, obligatory trendiness of his home page emerged in its proper milieu. In this new context, Ted's home page projects a message that the telco lab has up-to-date young Netheads from mit.

Although his presentation remains an outlier for his new work context, it carries the panache of his alma mater rather than the implication of a person acting out of synch with his environment. Interestingly, this explanation is self-contained in the page itself. Rather than just tell us about himself, which he does, Ted can also illustrate his sources and let them speak for themselves, so that we can interpret them as sources of influence on Ted; he does not have to tell us.

Ted's page led us, via the page of a colleague at mit, to Tabatha's. Tabatha works for a small software company, is very unconstrained in her presentation, and has succeeded in creating a real Net "identity" for herself, which has flooded out into print media discussions of Tabatha as an icon. Tabatha thus becomes a twice-removed social context for Ted. So if we think Ted is slightly outrageous for a telco lab, just look at his classmates' sites; and if they seem alternative, well, there is a pointer to Tabatha, the pace-setter. So we have the advantage of a much deeper context for Ted, and this is just going down one tree of his social links. Moreover, the richness of each of the sites on the path tells far more about him than he could express for himself. He is not those people. He does not have to state his membership explicitly—which would tend to cast it into an interpreted one-dimensionality—but he shows that he is part of that milieu.

In this we see a far more powerful social force than the decontextualization of identity described by Stone and Turkle. While we must consider the possibility that Tabatha is a constructed "persona," there are many clues on her page which render this unlikely. The more interesting fact is that the home page constructor has the ability to add context to the presentation of self, by allowing the visitor to "go to the places the owner goes to" and "see for him/herself" where the creator is "coming from."

The wider social context is displayed more fully and as a form of primary data rather than reconstructed in the individual's explanation of him or herself. This is postmodern, in the sense that the browser has access to a much broader text and thus is in a position to construct an independent interpretation of the page creator. It is also the opposite of the page creator's constructing different and separate selves, which by definition are out of context.

A distinction to be made is that between those sites that have a work context as a primary reference and those that have a topic context as a primary reference. The page host who works as a janitor at a church and keeps an obituary home page seems not to have physical groups for primary reference. His work contexts are thus not particularly defining, and his interests may find their focus in his home page information and communications with those who visit it. Some people may derive primary associations from their web relationships, while others are simply reflecting their primary associations in their links.

Gender and Assumed Contexts: Audiences and Security. Another tacit effect on the content of the home page is gender. Unlike an e-mail address, a home page is fairly easily traced to a location. Home pages tend to have more explicit information in them, and presenters often say where they live. We don't notice this on the home pages of men, but the fact stands out on the home pages of women and children.

Quite the opposite of the gender-mitigating effect of electronic media argued by Haraway and Stone, the home page dramatically highlights gender issues. The advice "don't give out your phone number to people you don't know" remains in many women's minds from adolescence. Yet we have home pages in which a little girl states the village in England where she lives and a single mother describes her Seattle suburb. What do we make of these apparent breaches of conventional security rules?

We must resort for an explanation to the lack of view the presenter has of the audience for the presentation. Many home pages seem to be written in a group context, addressed to a peer or colleague group, and presume the social conventions of those environments. The 8-year-old in the English village may walk to the grocer's on her own, something she would be unlikely to do in New York City. The self-presentation is made within the context of presumed social boundaries. These boundaries imply the safety of a social group.

Mary presented photographs of herself with her colleagues, on her own and at her desk. Her photo at her desk chair showed a casual unisex outfit and posture which one of us felt was an "among friends" pose and the other interpreted as a "come hither" pose. How many other interpretations might there be? She was photographed at work by a co-worker or photographer. The context was the workplace; this is reflected in the pose. The workplace is a "safe" place; this is also reflected in the pose. Yet the presentation context is the wider world: all www users. We know from publicity and from reading topic lists that this world spans a wide spectrum of values and lifestyles. The display of this private content in an unfiltered context seems to be the dilemma of both the appeal and the contradiction of personal home pages.

The dilemma: to be aware of all the negative possibilities would inhibit someone from entering anything but the most formal information on a home page. Yet the apparent promise is a wider extension of self, some more essential, less formal, more fully contextualized self. The interest speaks to social needs. However, the medium lacks the differentiators present in social domains: screens, gatekeepers, threshold behavior, and discriminating perceptions that tend to avert access by the wrong parties.

The security issue is, how much risk are people actually taking by not mediating the boundary between the physical group around them, for example, a work group, which may form a context for the homepage, and the lack of this group presence in the actual private life or home, where the same person can also be "found" ? The page creator is transposing domains, whereas in life they would differentiate between information conveyed in different domains.

Continuing Ambiguity of the Home Page

We have attempted here to bring forth a few of the issues that arose in looking at home pages as a presentation of self. First of all, counter to the multiplicity argument posited by postmodern cyberspace theorists, home pages attempt to construct a unified presentation or at least to pull together diverse aspects of the self so that browsers can follow paths that interest them.

Home pages tend to present social context by the fact of where they are located, especially if at a corporate site, or by the links they establish to other domains and other people. In this way they seem to be inherently social rather than focused on the individualism that is required for anonymous multiple presentations. Because they address an often presumed, yet unknowable audience, we perceive unresolved boundary issues in home page presentation, especially in the areas of personal disclosure and privacy and security awareness.

Although we have asserted that the home page is a pulled-together presentation of self, this does not mean that the self-presentation must be totally consistent. It is less audience selective than everyday life, and in this way, has the possibility to be a boundary-shifting medium which carries over into physical domains. Alternatively the home page may remain a unique venue for the more architectural metaphor of postmodernism: the mixing of styles and features from multiple conventions.

An important arguments concerning the nature of social activity on Internet. Because the case has been made with considerable persuasiveness that Internet is a place to explore alternate personae and abandon the political locatable individual, we felt the need to begin our discussion with a refutation of that case based in social theory and the logic of other phenomenologies.

The primary flaw is the conception that escape from the physical person is a desirable and rewarding activity which will set a cultural trend toward a decentralized self. By reviewing theories of coconstruction, which depend entirely on shared meaning, by establishing the primacy of the physical being and its historicity as the locus both of intelligence and of the social construction of self, and by showing the use of electronic media as just another tool toward general social purposes, we hope to situate Internet use in a broader and more continuous social context.

Finally, some of the distinctive features of personal home pages for the way they uniquely illustrate the effort to pull together a cohesive presentation of self across eclectic social contexts in which individuals participate. Rather than live as "fragmented selves," our home page presenters go beyond self-description to the illustration of their Net-linkable social contexts.

At the same time, many boundary questions are raised by the use of these media, and remain to be resolved as conventions applicable in one domain (physical social contexts) fail to translate to others. However, the resolution of boundary issues is part of the ongoing social process of contextualization and coconstructed self-presentation.

3

Computerisation in Ogranisational Context

Because of the powerful role that organizations of all kinds play in our society, it's important that we understand how they behave. The owners and managers of organizations often take organizations for granted. But many professionals are ambivalent about the roles of organizations in understanding how our society computerizes.

In a society in which many key goods and services are provided by organizations which employ hundreds to thousands of people — the airlines, state university systems, pharmaceutical firms, insurers, phone companies, hotel chains, automobile manufacturers, and so on.

Of course, many important life events do not take place in relationship to organizations — especially large ones. But from our births in hospitals to the recording of our deaths by county administrators, we deal continually with organizations. And the ways that these organizations computerize can influence the nature of their services, the costs of their goods, the ways that we interact with them, and their kinds of workplaces.

It is easy to refer to all government agencies as bureaucracies and emphasize their rigidities and rule-boundedness, while missing their roles as political agents which serve some interest groups more than others. It is easy to characterize private firms as efficient agents of their boards of directors, while underestimating the bureaucratic features of the larger firms. Or we might be willing to see a behemoth industrial firm like IBM as an arthritic bureaucracy, but miss the bureaucratic elements of more popular firms like Apple Computer or Ben and Jerry's ice cream company.

Business writers, managers, and technologists often argue that computerized information systems are essential if modern businesses are to compete nationally and internationally. In fact, some have argued that information technology and related skills are the new wealth of nations. The specific arguments vary, and focus on different aspects of organizational life. Some focus on the ways that computer systems help firms develop new services, while other arguments emphasize the ways that computerized systems might enhance workers' productivity. It is an important social choice to organize society so as to maximize efficiency and profit. The decisions to computerize are never merely economic.

In Getting the Electronics Just Right Barnaby Feder examines computerization at Wells Fargo, a major California bank. Feder's story concisely describes several different computerization efforts, some aimed at providing new services, and others aimed at improving internal efficiencies. Feder's account is one of the rare concise portraits of many different computerized information systems in a firm. Because of its brevity, it is necessarily highly simplified. Like many business writers, Feder stresses how a firm succeeded in developing innovative computer systems and new services. While each of Feder's descriptions portrays Wells Fargo as a cheerful place to work, one can readily imagine the stress that many workers felt in developing or using these information systems. Usually technological and organizational innovation is costly even when things go well.

In *How Information Technologies Can Transform Organizations*, Michael Scott-Morton of the MIT Sloan School examines how organizations can benefit from making major company-wide investments in networked computer systems and how they should align their approaches to computerization with other major organizational strategies.

"...information technology is a critical enabler of the re-creation (redirection) of organizations. This is true because it permits the distribution of power, function and control to wherever they are most effective, given the missions & objectives of the organization and the culture it enjoys.

"IT (Information Technology) is available to radically alter the basic cost structure of a wide variety of jobs, jobs affecting at least half the members of an organization. IT is only an enabler, however: to actually change jobs takes a combination of management leadership and employee participation that is, thus far, extremely rare."

"In summary, the traditional organizational structures and practices do not have to stay the same as we move into the 1990s. All dimensions of the organization will have to be reexamined in light of the power of the new IT. The economics are so powerful and apply to so much of the organization that one has to question everything before accepting the status quo"

Morton offers a relatively sophisticated conception of information technologies by viewing them as enablers rather than as causes. Morton is optimistic about the potential value of information technologies to upper managers and professionals, but he differs from the technological utopians by refusing to treat technology as a simple cause. He observes that effectively selecting, organizing, and using information technologies requires many subtle assessments of an organizations strategies, its culture, and the character of specific technical systems. He also notes that relatively few business firms have reaped broad benefits from IT. This is a frank observation to come from a senior professor of IT at MIT's Sloan School of Management.

Innovation is fraught with risks, and costs can escalate when things go wrong. And even very expensive projects developed by highly qualified professionals can fail to meet their designers' expectations; in extreme cases they may be aborted. Douglas Frantz examines how another major bank, the Bank of America, spent $60 million to get a $20 million computer system for trust-management to work properly — and then abandoned the whole project.

The Bank of America's experience is not unique. Many computerization projects lie between the Bank of America and Wells Fargo — they ultimately work in some way, but they take longer to implement, cost more, and are much more disruptive than their advocates had hoped. Since managers and professionals are usually embarrassed when their computerization projects do not go smoothly and according to schedule, few of the professional articles about computerization accurately portray the dynamics of computerization in real organizations.

The main controversies about the role of computer systems in supporting new services concern the extent to which they serve as economically effective means for drawing new customers, retaining old ones, and improving the economy generally. At the same time, computer-based services are not just conveniences. Their widespread deployment restructures industries, as well as relations between people and organizations.

The new groupware tools are so powerful, in fact, that they virtually compel companies to reengineer themselves. By giving workers well below the top of the organizational pyramid access to information previously unavailable or restricted to upper levels of management, groupware spreads power far more widely than before. Many who have grown comfortable dwelling near the pyramid's apex are understandably distressed by the way groupware disrupts old-style hierarchies.

Today's leaders in instructional computing favor an access model in which networked systems enable teachers and students to collaborate and gather information from distributed resources and communities of peers. Schools are lagging behind, though, in the critical area of curriculum development for using computer-based tools in subject matter classes. Most subject-matter teachers have not yet learned how, for example, spreadsheets relate to mathematics instruction, or multimedia to English or fine arts instruction, or databases to science instruction. For computer education to avoid becoming simply another isolated set of skills and procedures to be mastered, a major effort in curriculum upgrading must occur within the academic disciplines, as they are practiced in typical school settings.

Textbooks, paperbacks, blackboards, radio, film, film strips, airplanes, television, satellite systems and telecommunications have all in their time been hailed as modernizers of education. Technologies are social constructions (rather than contraptions or machines) which are value laden, and any practice (and a technology is, after all, a set of practices glued together by values) that threatens to disrupt this existing structure will meet tremendous resistance at both adoption and implementation stages.

The divergence of interests between managers and workers, and the potential implementation fissures along those lines, is a source of much of the implementation failure of widely-touted advances.

The technologists' rhetoric is remarkably consistent regardless of the specifics of the machine at issue. So too is their response when the technologies in question meet with only a lukewarm response: to blame the stubborn backwardness of teachers or the inflexibility and insularity of school culture. While elements of both of these certainly play their part in what I'll call 'technology refusal' on the part of schools, it behooves us to remember that all technologies have values and practices embedded within them. In this respect, at least, technology is never neutral; it always makes a difference. From this perspective, the reactionary response on the part of schools perceived by technology advocates makes a great deal more sense than the pig-headed Luddism so often portrayed. Further, technology refusal represents an immediate and fundamentally accurate assessment of the challenges to existing structures and authority that are embodied or embedded in the contested technology.

Hodas' paper provide a rich analysis of the ways that many interesting forms of computer-supported education threaten the expertise of many teachers' and thus a key aspect of their sometimes shaky authority. Hodas argument differs fundamentally from Becker's since he sees the core cultures of K-12 schools, rather than money, skill, and time, as the central dilemmas of effective instructional computing. Arguably the best examples of the effective integration of instructional computing can be found in colleges and universities rather than K-12 schools. How do the most lively colleges and universities differ from K-12 schools, beyond their abilities to accept and retain the more talented and motivated students and their relatively free intellectual milieux? Unfortunately, even the best universities have sometimes engaged in million-dollar instructional computing projects that had little sustained educational value.

Underlying these debates about computerization in banks, consulting firms, and schools is a deeper set of debates about how organizations behave with information technology. Feder, Kirkpatrick, and Becker tacitly work with a vision of organization which sociologists refer to as a Rational Systems model. A Rational Systems Model focusses upon clear goals, tasks, specialized jobs, and procedures (including information flows, authorizations, etc.). Concerns for efficiency dominate the organization, in this view. In contrast, Frantz, Orlikowski and Hodas work with a Natural

Systems model. Natural Systems Models focus upon the ways that work is done based on informal influence — including informal communication patterns, status, power, friendships, emerging roles, etc. Goals may be ambiguous, resources inadequate and problematic, and groups may seriously conflict within and between organizations, and act in self-interested ways to maintain their survival.

These different models lead analysts to have very different expectations of the roles of computer-based systems in organizations. Rational Systems analysts do not always see computerization in rosy terms, although they often do (e.g., Feder). Since Natural Systems analysts see large organizations as having multiple and conflicting goals, and as incapable of perfectly meeting any goal in a sustained way, they view computerization as much more problematic, even when it works well. Natural Systems models examine an information system that failed or computerization projects that have had limited success, other analyses from this perspective have examined how political action is critical for the success of information systems.

Since the 1970s a group of scholars including Bill Dutton, Suzanne Iacono, John King, Rob Kling, David Knights, Kenneth Kraemer, Kenneth Laudon, Lynne Markus, Wanda Orlikowski and Geoff Walsham, produced a series of detailed studies that examined how the political coalitions within organizations shaped decisions to computerize, and the consequences of computerization.

These scholars focussed on large organizations — with hundreds or thousands of employees. They found that these large organizations were frequently segmented into coalitions that held conflicting views of which goals the organization should emphasize and which strategies would best achieve them. While the computer projects favored by specific coalitions often had important elements of economic rationality, they often helped to strengthen the power of their champions as well. In fact, systems champions often exaggerated what was known about the economic value or necessity of specific projects. From this perspective, computerization entails organizational changes that do not benefit all participants. For example, in some research universities, the scientists have acquired relatively powerful "number crunchers", while instructional computing labs are relatively impoverished. Students and faculty do not necessarily benefit comparably when a university invests several million dollars in new academic computer systems. "Computer power" comes in part from the organized action of social systems rather than simply from "faster" computers with larger memories and greater communications capacity.

Those analysts who examine computerization from a rational systems perspective view computerization in very different terms from those who view computerization from a Natural Systems perspective. It is relatively rare that analysts of these differing persuasions debate each other. The controversies are much more implicit in the diverse stories about computerization, such as the contrasts between Kirkpatrick and Orlikowski or between Becker and Hodas. Newspapers and professional journals are most likely to publish systems rationalist accounts, while the natural systems accounts are most likely to appear in a small number of scholarly journals and books. While this is a critical controversy, the debate is not explicit and not joined.

Natural Systems analysts, like Hodas and Orlikowki, believe that behavior within organizations is really crucial for understanding the role of computerization in shaping organizations. In fact, some analyses within this approach examine computerized systems as forms of organization rather than as easily separable entities.

Computerization and the Productivity Paradox

Many analysts have argued that organizations could effectively increase the productivity of white collar workers through careful "office automation". There is a routine litany about the benefits of computerization: decreasing costs or increasing productivity are often taken for granted. For example, here is a brief sample news item from a computer science journal:

Chrysler Corporation's new computerized car design system promises to accelerate the development of cars by thirty per cent, saving the automotive giant millions of dollars in car costs. The $200,000 system was developed by the Evans and Sutherland Company of Salt Lake City.

Brief items like this appear frequently in newspapers and magazines. That they are often printed without comment — as statements of fact — indicates the way in which the link between computerization and cost-savings is often taken for granted. We might imagine some alternative news clips:

Chrysler Corporation's new air conditioning system in its design center promises to accelerate the development of cars by thirty per cent, saving the automotive giant millions of dollars in car costs.

Chrysler Corporation's new practice of having designers feel free to look at the ceiling when they let their minds wander promises to accelerate the development of cars by thirty per cent, saving the automotive giant millions of dollars in car costs.

These story-lines could have plausible rationales. Staring at the ceiling could free up the imaginations of designers; better air conditioning might improve their ability to concentrate during Detroit's hot, humid summer days. But stories like these are less likely to appear without some special explanation! The theme of computerization's direct economic value has already become a cultural stereotype in the United States. Like many stereotypes, it is based on some important insights. But like all stereotypes, it alters those insights and goes well beyond them.

Sometimes these stereotypes concerning the economics of computerization actually work against managers and their staffs. Some computer-based systems have enabled organizations to reduce the amount of direct labor required for certain everyday activities — such as calculating and printing routine bills. However, many computer applications improve the quality of the work done, rather than reduce the number of people who work in a specific office. And this result won't readily appear in cost-accounting.

For example, some computerized accounting systems provide more detailed, timely, and accurate information about expenditures than do their manual counterparts or simpler computerized precursors. Use of these systems can sometimes help managers and professionals to manage their funds better. But they may also require as many accounting clerks as the simpler systems for organizing data and producing new reports. Higher-level managers in organizations have sometimes balked at investing in more sophisticated computer applications and have refused to approve proposals for new computer systems without associated staff reductions. Many managers view computer systems in direct economic terms — in terms of money spent or saved, and revenues generated.

Concerns with economic costs and payoffs might appear as rather narrow and very concrete, in contrast to a richer array of social values which we examine elsewhere in this book. Even so, there is a substantial debate about why organizations adopt some computer-based systems and why they do not adopt others. For example, despite the routine claims that computer-based technologies decrease costs and raise productivity, it is remarkably difficult to find careful cost/benefit studies of computerization in particular firms.

Executives report that they do not evaluate IT on productivity alone, but that they also emphasize issues such as revenue stability, risk avoidance, growth potential, strategic flexibility, or market share. But productivity improvements are important at the level of the whole economy to increase the economic standard of living.

The meaning of productivity is much narrower than a "positive cost/benefit ratio," and the term productivity is often used inaccurately and very loosely. Productivity refers to a ratio of outputs divided by inputs. The outputs can be units of goods or services or revenue, and the inputs can include labor, equipment, supplies, and similar costs. For a simple example, consider an office assistant who is paid $6 per hour and who has an ink-jet printer that prints two pages per minute to help her produce ten two-page letters a week during a part-time job. If her supervisor bought her a $2,000 laser printer that printed 12 pages per minute, she would spend less time waiting for her letters to print. She would feel more productive since a letter would be printed almost as fast as she turned to the printer. In fact, she would be saving about 10 minutes a week in finger-tapping time, at a labor savings of about $50 per year. However, if she were the only person to use that new printer, the organization's productivity would have decreased, because the cost of producing each letter would have increased after we add in the cost of the laser printer. However, if 12 full time assistants who produced 40 letters each week were paid $12 per hour shared this faster laser printer, the organization could be more productive after two years.

Many of us feel more productive when we get more done, or seem to be wasting less time. We focus on outputs or the costs that we bear personally. But the economic measures of productivity are defined by ratios of outputs to total costs, and are very sensitive to labor rates, equipment costs, and similar factors. One of the complications in measuring productivity is that new equipment or technical systems can often produce qualitatively different kinds of products.

The 12ppm laser printer is not just a faster ink-jet printer; it is likely to store more varied fonts, print with much finer resolution, and consequently be used for printing niftier documents, like brochures and charts. These new capabilities sometimes give people a heady feeling of heightened effectiveness, and it has helped energize excitement about the economic value of computerization. But qualitative changes in the nature of computer-supported services make productivity comparisons more complex in practice.

One key point that is usually ignored is the way in which the burden for increasing productivity with computer systems usually falls on the poorest paid workers in an organization. A clerk who is paid $20,000 per year must increase her productivity five times as much as a $100,000 a year executive to get a comparable return on a $10,000 computer investment. Over a three year period, the clerk must increase her effectiveness (or productivity) by 15% a year (6 hours a week equivalent) while the executive need only improve by 3% a year to break even on the investment. Computerization is one strategy among many that organizations can employ to reduce costs or improve revenues and service. Other common strategies include improving the structure of the organization including reallocations of responsibility, reducing the levels of hierarch, reducing the amount of internal review and paperwork, etc. Computerization often seems most effective when it is coupled with a sensible reform program, rather than simply as a freestanding effort "to modernize."

The few systematic exceptions to this rule appear in some of the software reviews and advice sections written in popular publications such as PC World, Mac World, PC Magazine, and Byte Magazine, which sometimes identify clumsy features in commercial microcomputer software. But these reviews are exceptional, and are most likely to be read by computer specialists and computer buffs. And the names of some software packages, such as WordPerfect, RightWriter, Sidekick, and Excel, suggest graceful, refined tools that help only as needed.

It is common knowledge that programs can have bugs, or that people may have trouble transferring data between two different kinds of computers. But these problems are usually viewed as rare anomalies. An anomaly is an occurrence that differs from what one reasonably expects. Suppose that you write a report at home on a computerized word processor and take the file to your office for printing. If the system configurations in both locations are comparable, you naturally expect the report at work to print exactly as you formatted it at home; any differences appear to be anomalous.

Contrary to much advertising and reporting, problems in ordinary uses of computer systems can consume large amounts of time and patience.

The folk wisdom about computing is framed in a series of assumptions about the normal operation of equipment, such as that reports formatted on one microcomputer will print "properly" on another compatible computer which runs the same version of the software. The conventional wisdom of the computing world also has some general "escape clauses" — such as Murphy's Law. And the vision of computing advanced in many popular and professional sources is of a set of technologies which are easily usable, highly reliable, and relatively seamless.

In "The Integration of Computing and Routine Work", Les Gasser examined the way in which anomalies are common in the daily use of computing systems. Anomalies include system bugs, but they go much farther. For example, in 1990 the State of Massachusetts billed the city of Princeton, MA one cent in interest after it paid a bill for a ten cent underpayment of taxes. Each of these transactions cost twenty nine cents in postage, as well as several dollars in staff time and computing resources. The reporter viewed the situation as anomalous because one would not expect organizations to routinely invest many dollars in attempting to collect a few cents. However, the computer program was probably working as it was designed — to compute interest on all underpayments and produce accurate bills for interest due to the State of Massachusetts.

Table 1 Average Annual Growth in Gross Domestic Product per labor Hour

	Average Annual (% per) Growth Rate year)	
Sector	1948-1973	1973-1989
Business	2.9	1.1
Goods Producing	3.2	1.7
Farming	4.6	2.0
Manufacturing	2.9	2.8
Service Producing	2.5	0.7
Communications	5.2	4.6
Utilities	5.9	2.5
Trade (Whsl+Retl)	2.7	1.2
Finance/Real Estate	1.4	0.2
Services	2.1	0.3
General Government	0.2	0.3

In the last few years economists have found it hard to identify systematic improvements in United States national productivity which they can attribute to computerization. Although banks, airlines and other United States service companies spent over $750 billion during the 1980s on computer and communications hardware — and unknown billions more on software — standard measures have shown only a tiny 0.7 percent average yearly growth in productivity for the country's service sector during that time. Table 1 also shows that productivity growth in many sectors of the United States economy was much lower since 1973 than between the end of World War II and 1973.

The discrepancy between the expected economic benefits of computerization and measured effects has been termed "The Productivity Paradox," based on a comment attributed to Nobel laureate Robert Solow who remarked that "computers are showing up everywhere except in the [productivity] statistics." Brynjolfsson groups many of the explanations that have been proposed for the productivity paradox into four categories: errors in measuring organizations' outputs and inputs; lags in time due to the time that organizations need for learning about information technologies and adjusting to them; redistribution and dissipation of profits; and the systematic mismanagement of information and technology.

In the next three selections, Martin Neal Baily, Paul Attewell and John King all examine the last three of these explanations and different facets of the productivity paradox. Each of them tacitly relies upon Natural systems models of organizations in examining why business firms don't computerize in ways that significantly improve their overall productivity.

In "Great Expectations: PCs and Productivity" economist Martin Neal Baily, raises questions about the cost-effectiveness of many computer applications. Baily keeps his eye on the overall productivity of the U.S. economy, as measured by economists.

He notes that overall productivity growth in the U.S. economy has been very sluggish in the 1980s. While the aggregate statistics about productivity mask large variations among different firms, and even within particular firms, Baily wonders why the nation's major investment in computing technologies has not shown up in national level data.

Baily notes that computer systems often do things better than their manual equivalents. Computerized word processing systems make it easier than ever to revise a manuscript forty times, and financial analysts find it increasingly simple to break their data into finer slices and report them more frequently. But Baily notes that it is usually hard to place an economic value on more polished manuscripts and refined reporting.

He also questions the role of certain applications in altering productivity within firms or within an industry. He points out that systems that help a firm attract its competitor's customers may be great for the firm; but it doesn't raise overall economic productivity. As Baily asks at one point, somewhat rhetorically, "If this stuff is so good, why do we have the same number of secretaries?"

"Information technology and the Productivity Challenge," Paul Attewell reviews his own research to identify six common social processes which reduce the productivity gains from computerization. Attewell does not argue that computerization is inherently worthless for many organizations. Rather, he notes that many changes in products and ways of work that come from computerization, such as improving the appearance of reports and visual presentations or managers being able to rapidly produce fine grained reports about their domains of action, often do not result in direct improvements in overall organizational productivity. Numerous accounting reports may give managers an enhanced sense of control. But managers may seek more reports than they truly need, as a way to help reduce their anxieties about managing.

Similarly, some professionals may be specially pleased by working with advanced technologies. But much of the investment may result in improving job satisfaction rather than being the most effective means for improving organizational productivity.

Attewell does not argue that managers should not have some way of controlling activities for which they are responsible or that professionals should not enjoy their jobs. But he surmises that overall, a large fraction of the nation's multi-billion dollar investment in computerized systems have resulted in diverse changes which are "captured" within organizations rather than being translated into substantial overall productivity increases.

In "Where ares the Payoffs from Computerization?: Technology, Learning and Organizational Change" John King carries Attewell's argument further. He acknowledges that organizations may have not substantially improved their overall productivity because of their ways of computerizing. And he acknowledges the importance of social processes like those that Attewell identifies as turning computerization towards diverse ends. And he adds an important analysis of the ways that accounting and reporting organizational activities can confound our understanding of organizational productivity. But King's special advance beyond Attewell's argument lies in his historical argument about the organizational learning that is required for important innovations to effectively diffuse throughout industrial societies and for numerous mangers and professionals to figure out how to use them effectively. King's argument builds on the research of historically oriented scholars such as economist Paul David. David examined the replacement of steam driven factory equipment by electric motors in the early 20th century. While electric motors offered many advantages over steam, he found that it took over 20 years for the productivity gains of electric motors to show up in national level productivity data. King notes:

> If and when computerization yields major productivity payoffs it will be as a result of the confluence of three factors: The new technologies themselves, the know-how needed to apply them successfully, and the wholesale substitution of the new technologies and new methods for older ways of doing things. the new technologies are here, and it is clear that we are learning to apply the technologies, but we have not learned enough to achieve cost-saving substitution. We are still bearing the direct costs of learning, and we must bear the costs of multiple, redundant systems until we have learned enough to switch completely from the old to the new. This learning phenomenon might sound simple and straight-forward, but it is not. It is highly complicated and it takes considerable time.

Organisational Analysis in Information and Computer Science

During the last 30 years there has been a huge sea change in the nature of jobs for people educated in academic information science and computer science programs. To simplify, in the 1960s, most such people worked as software developers or support people for batch computer systems. The computer industry, aerospace firms, and large database providers were major sites of employment. Assembly language, COBOL and Fortran reigned supreme as programming languages. The concept of a "person who used their products" was usually an abstraction. In the 1990s, the spread of desktop computing and networks of all shapes and sizes has lead to a demand for people with information and computer science skills very close to the site of application. In the concluding selection, "Can Computer Science Solve Organizational Problems?," Many information science and computer science graduates need some skills in analyzing human organizations to do high quality professional jobs.

Organizational Informatics, to denote a field which studies the development and use of computerized information systems and communication systems in organizations. It includes studies of their conception, design, effective implementation within organizations, maintenance, use, organizational value, conditions that foster risks of failures, and their effects for people and an organization's clients.

4

The Network Paradigm

A new form of capitalism has emerged at the end of the twentieth century: global in its character, hardened in its goals and much more flexible than any of its predecessors. It is challenged around the globe by a multitude of social movements on behalf of cultural singularity and people's control over their own lives and environment. This tension provides the central dynamic of the information age, as our societies are increasingly structured around the bipolar opposition of the net and the self.

The net stands for the new organizational formations based on the pervasive use of networked communication media. Network patterns are characteristic for the most advanced economic sectors, highly competitive corporations as well as for communities and social movements. The self symbolizes the activities through which people try to reaffirm their identities under the conditions of structural change and instability that go along with the organization of core social and economic activities into dynamic networks.

New social formations emerge around primary identities, which may be sexual, religious, ethnic, territorial or national in focus. These identities are often seen as biologically or socially unchangeable, contrasting with the fast-paced change of social landscapes. In the interplay of the net and the self the conditions of human life and experience around the world are deeply reconfigured.

Social development is inseparable from the changes in the technological infrastructure through which many of the activities are carried out, since technology is society and society cannot be understood or represented without its technological tools. Social changes and technological changes are intimately related.

Since the industrial revolution, the prevalent mode of production in Western societies has been capitalism, embodied in a wide range of historically and geographically specific institutions to create and distribute profit. The modes of development, on the other hand, are the technological arrangements through which labor acts upon matter to generate the product, ultimately determining the level and the quality of the surplus.

The evolution of the capitalist modes of production is driven by private capital's competitive pressures. Modes of development, however, evolve according to their own logic; they do not respond mechanically to economic necessities.

Technological innovations emerge from the interaction between scientific and technological discovery and the organizational integration of such discoveries in the process of production and management. The evolutionary model of two separate modes bears some resemblance to Marxist theory formulated by Louis Althusser who introduced a similar distinction between the relations of production (classes) and the forces of production (technique.

Technological development does not completely mirror the economic process because the former is also influenced by other factors, for example, inventiveness and experiments with non-economic goals. The results of technological innovation open up new possibilities which may or may not be realized by social actors using them. There is a strong interaction between the two processes of invention and application, but they cannot be conflated into a linear dependence of one determining the other.

At the base of this reorganization is the pervasive implementation of technological innovation since the 1970s, clustering around the convergence of computing and telecommunication. After analyzing the history of the technology since the late 1940s and comparing it to patterns of development in the Industrial Revolution, information technology evolves in a distinctively different pattern than previous technologies, thus constituting the "informational mode of development": a flexible, pervasive, integrated and reflexive, rather than additive evolution. The reflexivity of the technologies, the fact that any product is also raw material because both are information, has permitted the speeding up of the process of innovation.

This self-accelerating process has created in about twenty years a new economic condition, the informational and global economy. This new economy is informational because the competitiveness of its central actors (firms, regions, or nations) depends on their ability to generate and process electronic information. It is global because its most important aspects, from financing to production, are organized on a global scale, directly through multinational corporations and/or indirectly through networks of associations.

This new global economy is more than just another layer of economic activity on top of the existing production process. Rather, it restructures all economic activities based on goals and values introduced by the aggressive exploitation of new productivity potentials of advanced information technology. Existing processes become either reorganized into new patterns, for example from national to transnational production, or repositioned vis-a-vis the new highly productive sectors. What differentiates the new global economy from the world economy of previous ages is that "it is an economy with the capacity to work as a unit in real time on a planetary scale".

The global economy is characterized by its interdependence, its asymmetry, its regionalization, the increased diversification within each region, its selective inclusiveness, its exclusionary segmentation, and, as a result of all those features, an extraordinarily variable geometry that tends to dissolve historical, economic geography. The global economy has been created under the drive of restructuring the capitalist enterprise since the 1970s and, with increasing pace, in the 1980s.

The new network enterprise is a phenomenon comprising not only shifting internal hierarchies, but also changing patterns of competition and cooperation across institutions. The network enterprise is "that specific form of enterprise whose system of means is constituted by the intersection of autonomous systems of goals".

The restructuring of western corporations into more networked businesses created new work and employment conditions: the *networker* and *flextimer* replaced the full-time employee.

The common theme underlying the diversity of regional and sectorial patterns of economic change is the incorporation of similar information technology into historically very different businesses. Its most distinct result is the emergence of the space of flows: the integrated global network.

It comprises several connected elements: private networks, company Intranets; semi-public, closed and proprietary networks such as the financial networks; and public, open networks, the Internet. Social organizations reconstitute themselves according to this space of flows.

The space of flows is made up of three aspects:

— *Technology*: the infrastructure of the network.

— *Places*: the topology of the space formed by its nodes and hubs. Hubs are defined by the network but link it to specific places with specific social and cultural conditions. Nodes are the "location[s] of strategically important functions that build a series of locality-based activities and organizations around the key functions of the network". The importance of hubs to produce the strategic functions of the network and of nodes to concentrate decision-making are at the core of the dynamic of global cities.

— *People*: The secluded space of the managerial elite commanding the networks, such as gated communities, exclusive social clubs, VIP lounges at airports and hotels that are almost identical around the world. Together these dispersed and interconnected spaces build the physical base for the social cohesion of the new elite.

The space of flows has introduced a culture of real virtuality which is characterized by timeless time and placeless space. Timeless time the dominant temporality in our society, occurs when the characteristics of a given context, namely, the informational paradigm and the network society, induce systemic perturbation in the sequential order of phenomena performed in that context. Examples of such perturbations are the effects of global financial turmoil on local communities or reorganization of a global corporation on any of its local branches.

The space of flows dissolves time by disordering the sequence of events and making them simultaneous, thus installing society in an eternal ephemerality. In short, anything can happen at any time, it can happen very rapidly, and its sequence is independent from what goes on in the places where the effects are felt.

The distinguishing characteristic of the space of flows is binary time and binary space. Binary time expresses no sequence but knows only two states: either presence or absence, either now or never. Within the space of flows everything that is the case is now, and everything that is not must be introduced from the outside: that is, it springs suddenly into existence.

Sequence is arbitrary in the space of flows and disorders events which in the physical context are connected by a chronological sequence. Binary space, then, is a space where the distance can only be measured as two states: zero distance (inside the network) or infinite distance (outside the network), here or nowhere. For example, when seeking information on the Internet, the crucial distinction is whether this information is on-line or not. The continent in which the information resides within the network is largely irrelevant.

Everything that is on-line is accessible: it is here, without distance. Everything that is outside the network is infinitely far away, completely inaccessible no matter where the network is entered; when someone puts it on-line, then it is suddenly here.

The global economy is concentrated in relatively few places, such as the Silicon Valley, Wall Street or the development zones in southern China, as its core activities become centered around the processing of immaterial, placeless information. Nevertheless, their logics are less and less determined by their history. This relationship most distinctly:

> "While organizations are located in places, and their components are place-dependent, *the organizational logic is placeless*, being fundamentally dependent on the space of flows that characterizes information networks. But such flows are structured, not undetermined. They possess directionality, conferred both by the hierarchical logic of the organization as reflected in instructions given, and by the material characteristics of the information systems infrastructure....The more organizations depend, ultimately, upon flows and networks, the less they are influenced by the social context associated with the places of their location. From this follows a growing independence of the organizational logic from the societal logic".

Increasingly, power is concentrated in the intricate space of flows, to the extent that "the power of flows takes precedence over the flows of power". The space of flows expresses the dominant social logic in the Network Society. Financial markets, for example, have turned into the central event of the new economy to such an extent that "all other activities are primarily the basis to generate the necessary surplus to invest in the global flows, or the result of investment originated in these financial flows".

While the dominant social logic is shaped by the real virtuality of the space of flows, people live in the physical world, the space of places. This "condition of structural schizophrenia", where two different spatial and temporal logics clash, introduces massive perturbation in cultures around the globe. People lose their sense of Self and attempt to reclaim their identity in new forms.

The increasingly vigorous articulation of resistance against and projects alternative to the logic of the space of flows empties out the legitimacy of the institutions of the political democracy. Three examples of resistance identity are chosen for their radical differences in context and goals: Mexico's Zapatistas, the American Militia groups, and Japan's Aum Shinrikyo.

While each movement reflects the historical differences of its constituency and the threats it perceives in the transformation of its specific social landscape, "they all challenge current processes of globalization, on behalf of their constructed identities, in some instances claiming to represent the interest of their country, or of humankind, as well.

Project identity is formulated by major pro-active movements: environmentalism, feminism, gay and lesbian movements. The latter three are jointly framed along the lines of the end of patriarchalism. They represent the conflictual and interrelated character of identity building.

The possible end of patriarchalism not only opens up new possibilities of self-determination, but at the same time provokes very vehement reactions to preserve what is perceived as threatened. There is no predetermined directionality in history. A fundamentalist restoration, bringing patriarchalism back under the protection of divine law, may well reverse the process of undermining the patriarchal family, unwillingly induced by informational capitalism, and willingly pursued by cultural social movements.

The classic embodiment of *legitimizing identity*, the nation state, is losing its power, although, and this is essential, not its influence. The loss of power stems from a loss of sovereignty, effected by the globalization of core economic activities, of media, of communication and, very importantly, the globalization of crime and law enforcement.

The most obvious example of the loss of sovereignty can be found in the currency exchange markets, which have, since the late 1980s, outgrown the capacities of the central banks to control them. They now link up national currencies. This enforces financial coordination undermining the possibilities of national governments to formulate independent economic policy.

As the former CEO of CitiBank, Walter Wriston, enthusiastically hails: "The global market has produced what amounts to a giant vote-counting machine that conducts a running tally of what the world thinks of a government's diplomatic, fiscal, and monetary policy. That opinion is immediately reflected in the value a market places on a country's currency".

Globalization has put the welfare state under double stress. Not only are national budgets tighter under the coercion of global financial markets, but also global firms can take advantage of cost differentials in social benefits and standards. As a result, "welfare states are being downsized to the lowest common denominator that keeps spiraling downwards.

Nevertheless, the nation state remains crucially important because it is still the only legitimized entity from which multilateralism can be built to address increasingly pressing global problems. However, this proves to be a dilemma. On the one hand, it increases the pressure on the nation state to effect decisions in the international arena and, on the other, it diminishes its credibility in the area of domestic policy by constraining it in an ever more restrictive network of global agreements.

The result is a crisis of political liberal democracy. The nation state loses its ability to integrate its own constituency, an integration which has been achieved through locally built instruments of the welfare state.

At the same time, the policy process disappears into an increasingly abstract arena of international organizations. The traditional institutions of democracy are caught in a fundamental contradiction. "The more the states emphasize communalism, the less effective they become as co-agents in the global system of shared power. The more they triumph on a planetary scene, the less they represent their national constituencies".

The more the nation state withdraws from its citizens, the greater grows the need to find alternative sources of identity. Trapped between the increased articulation of diverse, often conflicting identities and the need to act on a global scene, the traditional democratic institutions–the civil society–are being voided of meaning and legitimacy: they lose their identity. The power of the political democracy, ironically at the moment when it reaches almost global acceptance, seems to be inevitably waning.

The rise of informationalism in this end of millennium is intertwined with rising inequality and social exclusion throughout the world. Social exclusion is flexibly defined as the systematic inability of individuals or groups to access the means for meaningful survival.

While the historic causes for Africa and United States exclusion vary from case to case, they nevertheless form an entity, the fourth world, because they all entered the information age in positions in which their exclusion is reinforced by the structural dynamic of informationalism.

In the United States, for example, the emergence of the space of flows, using telecommunications and transportation to link valuable places in a non-contingent pattern, has allowed the reconfiguration of metropolitan areas around selective connection of strategically located activities, bypassing undesirable areas, left to themselves. This development started long before the rise of the network society.

However, it is the new ability to effectively switch off areas which are viewed as non-valuable from the perspective of the dominant social logic, embedded in the space of flows, which has created black holes of informational capitalism: regions from where there is, statistically speaking, no escape from suffering and depravation. However, not all actors in the fourth world are simply switched off from the centers of prosperity. Some of them have established, with a vengeance, a perverse connection through the global criminal economy. Crime is as old as humanity, but its global character is a new phenomenon.

Traditional, locally-rooted criminal organization, such as the Sicilian Mafia or the Chinese Triads have taken advantage of the technological and organizational opportunities provided by the new communication technologies. They have set up global networks. Joined by newcomers, such as the cartels of Colombia or the Russian Mafiyas, they now interconnect.

Around the globe, they flexibly traffic illegal goods–drugs, weapons, nuclear material, illegal immigrants, women and children, and body parts–as well as providing illegal services such as contract killing, blackmailing, extortion, and kidnapping. It all comes together in the $ 750 billion which are laundered in the global financial markets. It is not so much the existence of a shadow economy but rather the penetration of all aspects of legal economy and state institutions which is a new phenomenon. The global financial markets have been fueled by adventurous money seeking investment opportunities outside existing legal controls.

The societies of Japan, Russia, Italy and Colombia, among others, have been penetrated to their core by organized crime. The political processes are influenced through sheer violence, for example the killing of special investigators in Italy, or through more subtle forms, like corruption.

The global criminal economy is the phenomenon which has most successfully combined the two central aspects of the Information Age: the Net and the Self. Based on strong local identities, violently established and maintained, they have created a flexible global network of fast changing strategic alliances to exploit whatever opportunity arises.

Another, albeit unrelated aspect of the shift away from global dominance by the centers of Western culture is the emergence of leading informational economies in the Pacific Rim. In the case of Japan, the institutions of the state, and societies at large, face a crisis for the same reasons as those of the Western democracies. After World War II the Japanese state nurtured forms of industrial development that were globally competitive and supported the particularities of its traditional values: stability, homogeneity and cultural isolation, and strong patriarchalism. This system has come under double stress since the late 1980s.

To the extent that the Japanese multinationals have become truly global corporations, they have been disassociated from the Japanese national economy and the values expressed in it. Increasingly, the long-term stability of employment is not guaranteed. From below, a cultural change is in the making, generally more critical of traditional authorities and in particular of the repressed position of women in Japanese society. Together, the pervasive logic of the network society and the more pronounced articulation of new identities puts the system at large under increased stress. While the manifestations of the transformation are decidedly Japanese, many of its characteristics are related, not so much to Japanese history, but to the general tensions of the Information Age.

5

Internet Firewall

The generic term "firewall" is increasingly being used to describe the combination of hardware, software and management activities that are used to effect the policy. Internet firewalls are a means of protecting networks by implementing access control to and from the Internet. In practice this is achieved by controlling the means of communication between the two networks, the TCP/IP suite of protocols. describes a firewall as an approach to security. He uses the term firewall to mean the strategies and policies and the term 'firewall system' to refer to the hardware and software elements that implement the policy. It has been noted that in practice an Internet firewall is more like a moat around a castle than a firewall in a modern building.

A firewall system is a collection of components that is placed between two networks and possesses the following properties:

— All traffic from inside to outside, and vice-versa, must pass through it.

— Only authorised traffic, as defined by the security policy, is allowed to pass through it.

— The system itself is immune to penetration.

In other words a firewall system is a mechanism used to protect a trusted network whilst it is connected to an untrusted network. Typically, the two networks in question are an organisation's internal network (trusted) and the Internet (untrusted). But there is nothing in the definition of a firewall that ties the concept to the Internet. Although the majority of firewalls are currently deployed between the Internet and internal networks, there are good reasons for using firewalls when connecting any trusted network with a less trusted network, be it internal or external.

A firewall can enforce security policy. The firewall is the means by which the network access security policy is implemented. Internet services considered to be insecure can be restricted and access to or from certain hosts can be restricted.

A firewall can log activity effectively.

A firewall can limit your exposure to the untrusted network by controlling/restricting access to/from it to the level defined in the security policy. This includes controlling what users use the Internet for.

A firewall can be a focus for security decisions - a choke point. All traffic to or from the Internet must pass through it. By focusing defences on this point they can reduce internal system security overhead since they allow an organisation to concentrate security efforts on a limited number of machines.

Whilst firewalls provide good protection at the lower levels of the TCP/IP model, they provide almost no protection against higher level protocols.

Any data that is passed by the firewall still has the potential to cause problems which, were these to be exploited deliberately would be labelled as denial of service or data driven attacks. For example a firewall offers no protection against viruses contained in files transferred via ftp or as MIME attachment to an e-mail message.

A firewall can't protect against malicious insiders. A firewall cannot differentiate between hosts on the same side of a network therefore any Internet Host can spoof any other Internet Host and any internal host can spoof any other internal host.

A firewall can't protect against connections that don't go through it (i.e. backdoors). Firewalls can restrict the access to certain facilities and users will sometimes bypass the firewall to gain access to those facilities. A good example would be a firewall that didn't allow access to the World Wide Web.

Users on that network may establish point to point connections with an Internet service provider over a normal telephone line and introduce Internet connectivity behind the firewall. This type of threat can only be addressed by management procedures which are embodied in the organisations security policies.

A firewall can't protect against completely new threats if the security strategy is different from "deny everything unless specifically permitted." Again this is dealt with within the security policy by basing it on just such a strategy.

Components of Firewall

Packet Filters

A packet filtering system selectively routes packets between internal and external hosts according to rules that reflect the organisation's network security policy. Packet filtering may occur in a router, in a bridge, or on an individual host and operates at the network layer.

Screening Router

The type of router used in a packet filtering firewall is called a screening router. It is configured with rules to block or filter protocols and addresses and is installed at the external network gateway. Internal users usually have direct access to the Internet while all or most access to site systems from the Internet is blocked. However, the router could allow selective access to systems and services, depending on the policy. Inherently dangerous services such as NIS, NFS, and X Windows are usually blocked.

The screening router passes or rejects an IP packet based on information contained on the packet's header. The main information used is :

IP Source and Destination Address: By filtering packets on the IP source and destination address the screening router is able to effectively block access to or from any site or host that is not trusted.

TCP or UDP source and destination port: The screening router makes use of the TCP "well known ports" to permit, deny, or re-route access to particular Internet services. For example many firewalls block all inward traffic except for email by rejecting all externally sourced packets bound for any port other than port 25, the Simple Mail Transfer Protocol port. The screening router can also route all World Wide Web traffic to a particular host.

A screening router is also able to base routing decisions on information not found in the packet header, for example the source and destination interfaces.

A packet filtering router can implement either of the design policies discussed earlier, however it suffers a number of disadvantages:

— there is little or no logging capability. It is often therefore difficult for an administrator to determine whether the router has been compromised or is under attack;

— packet filtering rules are esoteric and difficult to test thoroughly, which may leave a site open to untested vulnerabilities;

— if complex filtering rules are required, the filtering rules may become unmanageable, and

— each host directly accessible from the Internet will require its own copy of advanced authentication measures.

These disadvantages become magnified as the security needs of a protected site become more complex and stringent. Screening routers alone are therefore considered to be inadequate for effective security and several firewall architectures, such as the screened host and screened subnet, have evolved to overcome these limitations. These provide additional security in packet filtering firewall implementations by utilising additional routers, hosts and perimeter networks. Before examining these architectures it will be useful to examine application level gateways, the means by which control of network traffic is extended from the network and transport layers to the application layer.

Application Level Gateways

Application level gateways are specialised application or server programs that run on a firewall host. These programs provide a safety barrier between the internal user and the Internet. Instead of connecting to the Internet directly with, say, a World Wide Web browser, the internal user connects to the application level gateway instead. The application level gateway then establishes the connection with the required world wide web server on the Internet and acts as a go-between for the session.

Application gateways operate at the application layer and can therefore provide access controls at the application protocol level and can handle store and forward as well as interactive traffic. The main disadvantage of application level gateways is that they require special purpose code to provide each service that is relayed. However, this means that they therefore implement a policy of "deny everything unless explicitly permitted" by default, which is often advantageous from a security perspective.

Application level proxies understand the application protocol and are therefore able to control the session based on the operations being requested. For example an application level proxy is able to block FTP PUT commands whilst permitting FTP GET commands. The custom application acts as a "proxy" between the client and the server. Because all data between the client and the server is routed through the application proxy it is able to both control the session and provide detailed logging. This ability to log and control all incoming and outgoing traffic is one of the main advantages of application level gateway.

Circuit Level Gateway

Another type of application level gateway is called the circuit level gateway. Circuit-level proxies do not interpret the application protocols but they authenticate the user before establishing the circuits. They relay packets between the two communicating end-points but are not able to do any additional processing or filtering based on the protocol.

The advantage of circuit level gateways is that they provide services for a wide range of different protocols however they require special client software that has had system calls replaced with secure equivalents from a library such as Socks. This re-introduces the problem that host based security does not scale well.

As the size of the network increases the task of managing secure clients ecomes increasingly time consuming and prone to error. In general application level proxies use modified procedures and circuit level gateways use modified clients.

Firewall Architectures

The packet filtering technologies that are used in screening routers provide an efficient and general way to control network traffic. They have the advantage that no changes are required to host or client applications because they operate at the transport and network layers.

Application level gateways extend control of network traffic to the application layer, and have the advantage that because they can understand the application protocol they can implement a finer degree of control and provide detailed logs. Firewalls bring these components together to provide extremely effective network based security control. To illustrate this, several "standard" Internet firewall architectures or configurations are presented.

Dual-Homed Host

The simplest firewall architecture utilises a dual homed host. A dual-homed host is a computer that has separate network connections to two networks. Such a host could act as a router between the two networks, however, this routing function is disabled when dual-homed hosts are used in firewall architectures.

Because the routing function is disabled the host isolates the two networks from each other whilst retaining the ability to see traffic on both networks. Systems inside the internal network can communicate with the dual homed host via one network interface, and systems on the Internet via the other, however these systems cannot communicate with each other directly.

In a dual homed host architecture the dual homed host itself is critical to the network's security. Such hosts are often referred to as Bastion Hosts in the firewall literature. A dual homed host can only provide services by proxying them. Where proxies are not available a screened host or screened subnet architecture provide extra options for providing new and/or untrusted services.

Screened Host

In this architecture, the primary security is provided by packet filtering and a bastion host sits on the internal network providing the required application. The screening router's packet filtering rules are configured such that the bastion host is the only host accessible from the Internet. Connections to the Internet may be routed through an application proxy on the bastion host, or in some cases, allowed directly through the screening router, depending on the network security policy.

The screened host architecture adds an additional layer of security to the dual homed host architecture, as an attacker has to first bypass the screening router, and then the bastion host. Noting that the screened host architecture may, at first sight, appear to be less secure than the dual homed host architecture. This is misleading as the dual homed host itself may fail in some unexpected way, and that the two are therefore as secure as each other in practice.

Screened Subnet

With both the dual homed host and screened host architectures, the trusted network is vulnerable if the bastion host is compromised. The impact of the bastion host being compromised can be reduced by isolating it on a perimeter network. The simplest way to provide a perimeter network is to add an additional screening router to the screened host architecture. This architecture is called the screened subnet architecture. The bastion host is then located on the perimeter network between the two screening routers.

An attacker that successfully compromises the bastion host now will only be able to access the perimeter net. The trusted network is still protected by the internal screening router. Whilst the attacker will be able to use packet sniffer software on the perimeter network, he will not be able to collect passwords for, or to examine sensitive files on, the trusted network unless these are passed via the DMZ, which is itself a security weakness.

Digital Video Analysis

The growth of multimedia information systems and the availability of low cost video capture systems is leading to a significant growth in the use of digital video eg on the WWW.

Digital television is also on the increase. Tools for handling digital video are in their infancy compared, for example, to tools for handling text. We now need tools to browse, retrieve and navigate through digital video and the use of content based techniques will offer a powerful alternative to methods which simply add text annotation to video files.

Techniques for processing and understanding images initially concentrated on the analysis of single images or stereo image pairs, but more recently substantial efforts have been made to develop schemes for analysing image sequences and video. Dynamic scene analysis is an important area of research in computer vision. Digital video analysis has many of the problems of image analysis but with the addition of temporal and audio analysis added in.

An added complication is that objects may change their shape and size as time progresses ie between frames because of 3-D rotation or movement towards or away from the imaging device. Objects may also enter or leave the scene or become occluded or cease to be occluded between frames.

One of the starting points for digital video analysis is to try and divide the video into a series of shots. This is sometimes referred to as video segmentation and in the following section some of the simple algorithms for video segmentation are reviewed.

Video Segmentation

A video sequence consists of many frames, these are the individual images, and are generally the smallest unit we are concerned with in a video sequence. A contiguous set of frames representing a continuous action in time and space is called a shot; For example, a camera following a car travelling down a road, or a fixed camera viewing a building with people walking past it. A collection of related shots is called a scene. i.e. news footage is usually a scene made up from a shot of the anchor person followed by several shots covering the actual news footage. A cut or transition is the point at which shots change within a video sequence. Such transitions can be grouped into the following categories:

— *camera break*: this is the simplest form of transition, when the current shot ends the next shot starts on the next frame - an instantaneous change;

— *fades and dissolves*: these transitions take place over a number of frames, i.e. a shot is slowly faded out to black, or one shot is faded out while another is faded in;

— *spatial edit effects*: these also take place over a number of frames. An example of a spatial edit effect is when the last frame of a shot slides out to the right of the screen, uncovering the next shot in the background; and

— *other approaches:* there is no set number of transition effects, newer and more imaginative effects are constantly being developed.

Video segmentation is the process of dividing a video sequence up into its component shots. All frames within a shot are generally very similar, or contain one or more objects that remain visible throughout the shot. By contrast, consecutive frames on either side of a camera break are usually very different.

Therefore, if a quantitative measure of the qualitative difference between such frames can be obtained, this measure can be used to indicate whether a transition has occurred or not. The problem is therefore one of finding a suitable metric for measuring these differences. There are two commonly used metrics for detecting transitions:

— those based on measuring differences between corresponding pixels or block regions between frames;

and

— those based on global representations such as colour or intensity histograms of the frames;

There are other methods which use information extracted from compressed video data such as MPEG, to segment the video stream.

Pixel Difference Methods

Pairwise Comparison

The simplest method for calculating a difference between consecutive frames is to compare each pixel in one frame with the corresponding pixel in the next. If more than a certain percentage of pixels have changed between frames, then a shot transition is declared.

The major problem with this method is that it is very sensitive to camera and object motion. If the camera pans in any direction, even if only by a few pixels, then the majority of the pixels compared will be judged as different by the above metric. One solution is to smooth the image, so that each pixel has, for instance, the mean value of its 8 nearest neighbours. This also filters out some of the noise in the images, but still only compensates for minor camera or object motion. A better method is to compare block regions, rather than individual pixels. In this case, the metrics for deciding whether a change has occurred are based on the various characteristics of the regions.

Histogram Based Methods

Possibly the most popular method for detecting transitions is by comparing the intensity or colour histograms of consecutive frames. The theory is that two frames which have a common background and unchanging objects will show little difference in their histograms.

The comparison can either be on the global histogram, or local histograms, by splitting the images into smaller regions. The basic formulation for histogram comparison is as follows. The histogram (either colour or gray scale) is computed for each pair of consecutive frames.

Determining a threshold is again a problem, S.Devadiga proposed a video segmenting method called Hierarchical histogram-based video indexing (HHBVI), which segments a video into several levels of granularity by using varying values for the thresholds. This can be used to produce a tree structure with the root node pointing to the whole shot, down to leaf nodes pointing to sub-shots.

Another problem is that of a shot which contains rapidly changing frames - for instance, a strobe lighting effect - we as viewers may consider such a sequence as a single shot, but to the above algorithms it will be interpreted as many differing shots. Their solution is simply to put a constraint on the minimum length of a shot, thereby grouping a fast changing sequence of frames into a single shot.

By comparing only consecutive frames, transition effects such as fades and dissolves may be missed. H.Zhang et al have implemented a multi-pass, twin-comparison algorithm to overcome this problem. The main disadvantage of this algorithm is that although it detects gradual transitions well, it also identifies some camera operations such as panning, zooming, and tilting as false positives. The solution is to detect the camera operations directly.

Hirzalla and Karmouch detect the simple camera operations by looking at the hue flow pattern between consecutive frames, and comparing this to patterns formed by right-left panning, up-down tilting and in-out camera zooming operations.

H.Zhang et al.'s parsing system detects camera operations through motion field analysis. Zhang's technique is also a multi-pass method, in the first pass temporal resolution is sacrificed to detect potential transitions.

Optical Flow and the Motion Field

Optical flow is the apparent motion of brightness patterns across the image plane of a computer vision system or across the retina of the eye in a biological vision system. Optical flow arises from movement of objects in the scene or from movement of the camera (or eye) through the scene. It can also occur as an artefact of the movement of light sources illuminating the scene. The optical flow field is a vector field representing the optical flow at each point in the image.

The motion field is a field of vectors representing the motion of real world object points projected onto the image plane. In many cases the optical flow and the motion field are the same or very similar, but they can be quite distinct in specific circumstances.

B.K.P.Horn demonstrated this by considering a smooth metal sphere illuminated by a single light source and spinning on its axis. If the sphere is very smooth there will be no change in the brightness pattern and the sphere will appear to be stationary. Thus, the optical flow field is zero although the motion field is non-zero. If the same sphere is stationary but the light source moves so that the highlights on the sphere move, the optical flow is non-zero as the brightness pattern is moving even though the motion field is zero.

It should be noticed that it is the optical flow field which is observable in an image sequence although in most image sequence analysis it is assumed that the motion field and the optical flow field are the same. Calculating the optical flow field is the starting point for many motion studies in computer vision. If the camera is stationary and a moving object is assumed to be rigid, the motion field may lead to estimates for the relative depth of points on the object and hence provide a cue to the 3-D structure of the object. This is called structure from motion.

If an identifiable part of the scene is stationary but the camera is moving, the optical flow may lead to an estimate of the real world (3-D) motion vectors for the camera and this in turn may lead to estimates of the 3-D motion of any moving objects in the scene. Calculation of the optical flow is also used as a cue to aid the process of video segmentation.

6

Electronic Journals

Scholarly publishing in books and journals, like lecture series, workshops and conferences, are forums for scholarly communications whose character can be influenced by the media of communication. With each electronic invention, many scholars hope that new media can expand authors' or speakers' abilities to reach new audiences. They hope that listeners or readers will hear new voices, or hear old voices faster or more conveniently.

This chapter offers a way to conceptualize scholarly publications that can help understand some key issues in the debates about the appropriate roles of paper and electronic publication. It also examines some key beliefs that appear in the debates about electronic publication. One one hand, advocates of electronic publication often hold that paper- based journals (and books) will become obsolete within a few decades, that materials will remain in electronic form once they are in electronic form, that electronic publication offers an exceptional opportunity to speed and expand the range of scholarly communication, and that the shift to scholarly electronic publication is inevitable.

Few critics of electronic publication express their misgivings in writing, and dismiss these publications through indifference. But many scholars who are wary of electronic publication seem to think that the intellectual quality of electronic publications must be deficient in some key ways (in contrast with paper-based alternatives).

For simplicity, we will define an electronic journal (e-journal) as one which is distributed to most of its primary subscribers in electronic form. In contrast, a paper journal (p-journal) is one that is distributed primarily in paper form. It does not take much work to find that the number of e-journals is growing annually and includes fields from theoretical computer science to medieval literature, or to find numerous instances where scholars have learned of new results or studies more rapidly by using electronic media.

The more difficult questions are how to conceptualize the changing scholarly communications systems and their social roles. We are especially concerned about the next few decades — a period of experimentation, excitement, confusion, and anxiety — or the publication forms that thrive in this period may become institutionalized as the most valid forms of scholarly journals for the following century.

We will examine what we believe are the range of plausible forms of viable scholarly publishing, rather than emphasizing the most exciting but more socially fragile possibilities of electronic publication.

Scholarly Communication Systems are Socio-Technical Systems

While few scholars have diverse experiences with electronic publishing, academics are familiar with oral forms of scholarly communication, and its alteration by electronic communication. Amplifiers in lecture halls, video conferencing, and videotape alter the nature of audiences that scholars can reach, and also shift the relationships between those audiences and lecturers/ speakers. These electronically enhanced forums do not simply provide "more communication," but also alter the ways that people speak and interact. As the audience scales up in size, or moves out in space and time with real- time video or othertime video-tape, the informal give and take between speakers and listeners becomes more difficult (in contrast with the smaller face-to-face seminar). On the other hand, people watching a videotape may privately replay sections to enhance their comprehension, while in a face to face meeting they may have to ask questions (that might also embarrass the speaker or questioner).

Voice-based face-to-face conference, video conferencing, and videotape are not simply technologies; they shape scholarly communications as socio-technical systems in which social characteristics such as controls over access (via pricing and distribution channels), and social protocols for regulating discussions between speakers and audience also influence character of scholarly communications. The nature of videotape pricing and the distribution channels can lead to minor or huge expansions beyond the original conferees. Despite scholars' potentially broader access to conference talks via videotape distribution, a face-to-face conference is different from a videotape collection of its talks because of the diverse informal discussions and important social networking that conferences support. The face-to-face conference and the videotape collection are different scholarly communication systems with overlapping capabilities, but which also support very different forms of scholarly communication. These observations discourage us from conceiving of electronic media in exclusively celebratory, cornucopic, technologically utopian terms.

In a similar way, a scholarly journal can also be usefully understood as the product of a socio-technical production and communications system. The publishing communication system includes both full-text materials (articles and books), and indexes/pointers to these materials (including book reviews, abstract sets, specialized bibliographies, and diverse catalogs).

Most readers of p-journals see few of the social and technical alternatives that differentiate one journal's production and distribution systems from another's. Scholars are aware of different reviewing practices of journals in which they publish, and also aware of the time periods between the date that they send a final manscript to a publisher and the date that it appears in print.

But other differences in the production systems that create a journal's issues can also be substantial, and have been changing over time. Some scientific journals print color plates of a kind that were implausible twenty years ago, while many mathematics and humanistic journals still print exclusively black and white text and diagrams. Most p- journals are now willing to accept the final form of manuscripts in electronic form, and a few require it.

Further, some p-journals are willing to review articles that are submitted in electronic form. The production of scholarly journals has become much more computer intensive in the last decade, and there has been no significant scholarly controversies over these shifts. However, the possibility of electronic distribution — the distinguishing characteristic of e-journals — is the one that is most subject to debate by both publishers and scholars. E-journal editors and publishers have been experimenting with different ways to charge for an e-journal (now often free), have articles reviewed, layout each issue, and distribute it. We will discuss some of the differences in the socio- technical design of e-journals below.

Connection Authors and Readers

Scholarly publishing should be viewed as one part of the scholarly communications systems that connect authors and readers. In the extremes, world-class scholars (and national class scholars) are eager to have their works be read (and appreciated) by their peers, and also by some larger disciplinary or cross-disciplinary audiences that usually number in the range of hundreds to thousands. In contrast, there are other scholars who are simply happy to publish periodically, or at least publish before receiving tenure or other professorial promotions. Scholars are very sensitive to the legitimacy and status of the journals (or publishing houses) that publish their work, but they vary in their insistence in publishing in the journals that their peers regard most highly.

Every major traditional field has a few high status journals whose content is controlled by a small set of gatekeepers and is widely read within its scholarly community. Other journals that are believed to be of lesser quality and at the bottom tier are "write only journals" that few scholars read regularly.

Within the United States alone there are over 2,000 four year colleges and universities, of which fewer than 200 have vigorous campus-wide research programs. A relatively small fraction of 500,000 professors in the U.S. publish routinely in the highest status journals in their fields. The majority of professors publish relatively few scholarly works, and in the lesser quality journals, especially after receiving tenure. But even in many of the 1,800 colleges and universities with minimal research programs, faculty are often required to publish some work as a criterion for tenure. Some analysts would draw the boundary between these two classes more narrowly, and refer to perhaps 100 research intensive universities and 1900 other colleges and universities. Regardless of where one draws such boundaries, there is tremendous heterogeneity within these classes and a huge cultural divide in the meanings of scholarly publishing between them.

While communication systems link people (or groups), not every scholar writes to be widely read. They may publish so as to be seen as "being in the scholarly system" by their colleagues and academic administrators who review them for promotions and pay raises. In contrast, scholarly readers are usually seeking highly trustworthy or "interesting" materials within what they see as a huge corpus of publications (books and articles with plausibly relevant titles.) Scholars who work within well-defined article-based disciplines report that they routinely read a few "high-quality" journals (or conference proceedings). They find other works through diverse socially filtered processes that emphasize the credibility or "quality" of the work such as asking expert colleagues for references to related studies, tracing references in the bibliographies and footnotes of "high quality studies," or seeking the relevant publications of respected scholars.

Scholars often use electronic indices and abstracts to facilitate parts of these searches, especially when they are searching for a specific document or its location, based on clues about the author or title. These electronic indices and abstract services have expanded greatly in the last decade, and there is a good chance that they will continue to expand. For example, journal publishers may post their own journals abstracts on the WWW (or other services), although field-wide abstracts (ie., Chemical Abstracts) will probably remain viable for-profit independent services. Conference organizers may also post paper abstracts and author contact information on the WWW, and thus enable many potential readers to track parts of a field or to contact authors for specific papers (which they might send electronically or in paper).

But social networks also play a key role in informal scholarly communication. Scholars usually track the work of 10-50 colleagues (or labs). They often learn about new studies and results in their immediate areas well before they are published — through collegial conversation, conference presentations, attending invited seminars, acting as journal editors and reviewers, and receiving manuscript drafts or preprints from close colleagues. Active scholars are usually well positioned in these (primarily) verbal networks.

We have heard active scientists criticize p-journals because they print "old news" in fast moving fields when the publishing delays are one to three years between the time that an article is accepted and it appears in print. High energy physicists have taken a lead in developing a preprint server Hepnet where physicists can post articles that have been submitted for publication (articles are removed after they have been published). According to Stevan Harnad 25,000 physicists worldwide are accessing the archive 45,000 times a day, with 350 new papers deposited per week. Computer scientists have at least two networks of technical report search systems that can help eager readers locate papers when they are issued in the technical report series of the computer science departments at the major research universities.

Journals continue to play many key roles in scholarly communication, in helping ensure that published work is of higher quality than under a self-publishing system, resolving "priority of discovery" disputes, and in making work available to those who are outside of the tiny subcommunities that produce the leading work on narrowly defined topics. The journal system of scholarly publishing also seems to work as an efficient system of packaging materials and signalling the likely quality of the edited articles (as with brand names).

Economic Conditions and the Shift from Paper to Electronic Publication

To the extent that journals reflect the worldviews of their editorial boards, they also serve as relatively closed communication systems which innovate slowly. The most common conception behind new journals is the rise of new topics and new fields. But another key incentive for starting a new journal comes when a scholarly subcommunity has trouble getting its form of research published in highly legitimate or trustworthy journals.

The emergence of e-journals is driven by a few large scale social forces, above and beyond the technical capabilities and allure of low cost electronic distribution. Some of these include the continuing downsizing of US university budgets (relative to inflation), with a consequent flattening of growth in academic library budgets. At the same time, the costs of subscribing to scholarly journals has been generally rising much higher than inflation, with the largest price increases coming from for-profit European scientific publishing houses. These increases have been partly driven by the declining value of the US dollar against Western European currencies, and partly by increases in the cost structure of the publishing houses.

These economic conditions influence the nature of academic journals, as well as their circulation. The price of journals is highly correlated with their page counts, and both scholarly societies and trade publishers have been reluctant to increase page counts and prices, independently of the scholarly dynamism in the fields covered by a journal. Academic libraries have been cancelling journal subscriptions (but generally shifting their materials acquisitions budgets from acquiring monographs to maintaining journal subscriptions).

These economic conditions make it harder for scholars who want to initiate new journals to develop a workable circulation. Academic (and sometimes industrial laboratory) libraries are a major subscription base for scholarly journals. But when libraries are cancelling subscriptions, scholars face an uphill battle in having their library add new journals. Some university libraries are marked by the balance in their collections between old and new journals: they have respectable collections of established journals, but relatively few subscriptions to newer journals. This balance can undermine their abilities to support scholarship and teaching in new or emerging fields.

These conditions could also foster the development of e-journals, but e-journals have not yet become legitimate publication outlets. As with paper publications, articles that are submitted to e-journals may be lightly edited or tightly reviewed by an editorial board with strong academic standards. Today, many scholars are confused about the formats and intellectual quality of e-journals. In extreme cases, they feel that e-journals must be of lower intellectual quality than p-journals, because they sense something insubstantial and potentially transient — ghostly, superficial, unreal, and thus untrustworthy — in electronic media. In practice, some refereed e-journals publish high quality articles, but they are not well known by their existential critics.

E-Journal Formats

E-journals are not all alike. Like p-journals, they differ in the care with which their editors (and editorial boards) review papers. But they also differ in the way that they format articles for distribution and their actual distribution channels. We believe that the ways that e-journal editors design these aspects of their journals influences their likely acceptability by productive scholars, and thus their overall legitimacy.

In numerous conversations and interviews with diverse academics and librarians, we have heard some significant and common (but not universal) confusions about the nature and meanings of electronic publication. Scholars who do not work routinely with electronic texts often assume that they are deficient in some ways. For example, in when the editorial board of the ACM's Transactions on Information Systems (TOIS) discussed various formats for an electronic alternative, e-TOIS, in 1994, a mathematician colleague of one editorial board member sent a note which stated that "an electronic journal must be deficient in every way when compared with a paper journal." It is ironic that some of the editorial board's discussion was how and whether to make the e-TOIS superior in some ways to p-TOIS (for example by including more artwork, sets of data, and electronic pointers to related research).

One of the remarkable features of today's e-journals is that few of them use special features of the electronic media to scholarly intellectual advantage. Most of the e-journals publish papers that could appear in p-journals. In contrast, the Journal of Current Clinical Trials creates hypertext links between related articles and also letters to the editor related to specific articles.

Computer scientists have speculated about including executable algorithms and data sets with e-journal articles. And it might happen in the (electronic) Chicago Journal of Theoretical Computer Science. But, today, the articles that appear in e-journals, such as PostModern Culture, Electronic Journal of Sociology, Electronic Journal of Virtual Culture, and Public Access Computer Systems Review (and so on) do not make special use of their electronic formats, except for distribution.

With a few exceptions, e-journals exist in a kind of ghostly netherworld of academic publishing. As we mentioned earlier, university librarians seem puzzled about how to integrate them into their collections and how to provide them to their clients. They are not (yet) indexed in the Science Citation Index (with the exception of the Journal of Current Clinical Trials, the Social Science Citation indices, or in abstracting services such as MLA Abstracts or Sociological Abstracts.

One e-journal is worth singling out for attention because of its sociologically clever formats. The Journal of Artificial Intelligence Research is a relatively new e-journal that publishes its articles in electronic form, in Postscript, on WWW, gopher, and ftp servers when they are accepted for publication. The title and abstract are also posted on a Usenet newsgroup,comp.ai.jair.announce and also available on the Usenet newsgroup comp.ai.jair.papers. JAIR's editors offer authors the promise of rapid international access to their articles. Each article is formatted and paginated as it would appear in a printed journal. Someone who prints the Postscript file has an article which looks like the photocopy of an article from a traditional p-journal. A publishing house, Morgan-Kaufman, also sells a printed version of the journal in an annual issue to libraries and others, so that librarians can readily integrate Journal of Artificial Intelligence Research into their catalogs and collections.

JAIR as the Stealth E-journal of Artificial Intelligence Research. Its editors cleverly exploit the broad rapid international distribution afforded by Internet services such as WWW, while simultaneously calming authors' fears of publishing in a stigmatized electronic medium because it always looks like a p-journal and can be purchased in paper form. In fact, JAIR's editors encourage readers to cite articles published in JAIR in the same format that they would cite a p-journal article (and they do not encourage citations to include URLs).

The case of the Journal of Artificial Intelligence Research illustrates many key social features of electronic scholarly publishing. By publishing polymorphously in paper and electronic media, this journal can offer an electronic edge to authors while appearing traditional to those who do not know its workings.

Its authors and readers are part of a scholarly community where there is strong consensus on a computerized typesetting format (in this case Postscript), and in which every research lab has free (or subsidized) electronic access to Internet services. And JAIR is allied with a (commercial) publisher that routinely markets and sells books to libraries, scholars and professionals. One other key feature of JAIR's stealth approach is that it doesn't broadcast its e-journal status in its name. It is a fascinating model.

A few e-journals are affiliated with publishing houses that sell paper versions of the journal in annual bound volumes. We suspect that these e-journals which distribute both e- journal and p-journal versions have greater chance of being seen as legitimate publication outlets than those e-journals that distribute only in electronic form.

However many of these e-journals, such as the Public Access Computer Systems Review distribute their electronic articles as ASCII text. When they are printed for extended reading, annotation or distribution to colleagues, they do not appear to be neatly formatted bone fide journal articles.

In contrast JAIR takes an important step beyond that of most e-journals that also distribute and sell paper annual volumes by insuring that every printed copy of a JAIR article appears as a visually well-crafted facsimile of a photocopied journal page — complete with headers, footers and the specific page numbers for each article as they will appear in the paper volume that Morgan-Kaufman sells to libraries. JAIR leaves no traces of its e-journal status for academic administrators such as department chairs and deans to sneer at. If they see a JAIR article during an academic career review, it appears as a bone fide p-journal publication, and can be assessed on the basis of its content.

Some of these serendipitous enabling conditions that help link authors and readers may be found in some other fields, such as mathematics, where LaTex is a typesetting standard and where the active researchers also have Internet access. In many field, posting articles in multiple print formats — WordPerfect, RTF, and MS-Word — would probably make them accessible to most readers.

JAIR was able to become a legitimate computer science journal by through a clever set of conventions that hides its e-journal status. However, it can attract good authors by offering the advantages of rapid publication and a startegy of avoiding any stigma of e-publishing.

JAIR also allows authors to include elaborate appendices that can contain executable computer porgrams and data that are not published in the paper version. But aside from these optional appendices, JAIR's articles appear like traditional p-journal articles. The disadvantage of the JAIR format is that it doesn't allow articles to utilize key features of electronic publishing, such as hypertext within articles.

Once an Electron, Always an Electron?: How Do Media Matter?

University libraries have not yet developed ways to effectively archive e-journals and integrate them into their catalogs and collections, unless they can buy paper versions (as with JAIR, Public Access Computer Systems Review, etc.). There are serious questions about what a library should deliver when a client requests an article from an e- journal — a printout, a file, or a URL, for example. In a seminar in 1993, Rob Kling suggested that libraries print e-journals and integrate them into their paper collections. A librarian sternly informed him that a paper version of an e-journal "undermined the concept" of an e-journal.

In principle, paper and electronic media need not influence the scholarly quality of a book or journal. But paper and electronic media do have significantly different material properties, and that influences some of their social properties. It is usually easier to transform an electronic document into a paper form, than vice versa. In practice, paper and electronic formats have complementary virtues and vices. A key point is that most scholarly documents that start in electronic form will end up in paper form sooner or later. When publishers or readers (and their assistants) transform electronic documents into paper is part of the story of electronic publishing.

Fifty years ago, most scholars worked from longhand notes and manuscripts. In the 1940s to 1970s, many scholars developed typing skills and transformed rough notes and verbatim manuscripts from long hand to typescript. Some scholars composed on a keyboard. In the 1980s, many scholars began using word processors in lieu of typewriters. Scholars vary in the extent to which they start a manuscript by composing on keyboards or develop notes, outline or even a first full draft in longhand. Today, virtually all scholarly manuscripts exist, in part, in electronic form in a scholar's office. Pictures and diagrams are least often in electronic form, and the frequency of pictures and diagrams in a book or article varies a lot by discipline and subfield.

Even when scholars prepare papers and books in electronic form, they commonly print intermediate drafts for their own review and revision. Most scholars find it much easier to annotate paper manuscripts than electronic drafts. Paper manuscripts offers different affordances than electronic formats: ease of getting a sense of the whole, ease of short marginal comments and arbitrary markings, and portability. In contrast, electronic documents can be more rapidly searched for keywords and radically restructured. These complementary properties of paper and electronic documents also influence readers and well as authors. When academics obtain documents in electronic form — drafts, preprints, technical reports, and whole articles, they may preview them on screen. But in our research, they universally report preferring to print manuscripts for serious reading and annotation.

Collaborating co-authors may prefer paper formats for reading and electronic documents to facilitate revision. But other than authors, few scholars have a deep interest in revising the works that they receive!

That scholars in diverse fields will continue to write and revise their manuscripts while shifting back and forth between paper notes, electronic documents, and printed drafts read and marked for revisions. The existence of electronic documents heightens the possibility that they could be readily published (and distributed) in electronic form at lower costs to wider international audiences.

Scholarly book and journal publishers vary in the extent to which they will accept electronic submissions of original manuscripts, although the publishers are drifting towards accepting (or even preferring) electronic final copies in addition to a printed version.

Electronic documents do not remain in electronic form, and discussions of electronic publishing should be cognizant that exclusively electronic representations will be relatively rare in serious scholarly publications. Even so, there is a continuing slow shift from exclusively paper to a mixture of paper and electronic publishing, distribution, archiving, searching and previewing scholarly journals.

Field Shifts

Some key technological demographics will change considerably in the next two decades. More colleges and universities will wire many more of their faculties' offices and labs, although some campuses face daunting costs and complexities in cabling older stone buildings or cabling scattered buildings in dense urban districts.

Despite a cornucopia of new information that might be rapidly accessible, scholars will still work and live within a 168 hour week that does not expand. Active scholars often work sixty to seventy hour weeks, and are mindful of their time. Their attention is a precious resource. And publications in which editors or indexers help them focus on what they believe are the highest quality articles and reports are now and will remain at a premium.

We suspect that there will be many more electronic indexing systems that help point scholars to paper-based journals and conferences. We did not cover the sharing of datasets and software, but it is likely that there will be more specialties in which scholars share these costly intellectual resources via computer networks (much in the way that molecular biologists within very specialized communities use FLYBASE, GENBANK, and the Protein DataBase). Doubtless, more scholars will post preprints and reprints of articles on services like the World Wide Web (WWW). But will scholarly electronic publishing become legitimate and routine in this same time frame?

Andrew Odlyzko argues that the demise of p-journals is inevitable, and Harnad argues that academics should immediately abandon p-journals and publish in e-journals. These arguments focus on the technical process and economic costs of distributing e-journals (in contrast with paper). We have tried to locate journal publication within a larger social system of scholarly communication. And, within this frame, the rapid demise of p-journals seems less likely. We are am specially impressed by the way that molecular biologists who routinely share DNA sequences via genbank circulate paper preprints rather than electronic preprints. This might be a technological peculiarity which will shift as soon as 1200 dpi printers cost as little as a Laserjet (or Laserwriter). But there are deeper social relationships in scientific communities that influence these patterns.

Most academics now view electrônic publishing as experimental, at best. The segregation of e-journals into an electronic space that isn't (yet) integrated into the scholarly document systems of libraries, indices, abstracting services, and so on is a formula for continued marginality. In addition, commercial publishers are only cautiously experimenting with allowing the full text of p-journals to be licensed for electronic access (as in Elsevier's TULIP project).

All paper-based publishers are wary that unlimited on- line access to journal articles will erode their subscription base, and they have not yet developed good electronic subscription models to supplement paper publication. Scholars are used to unlimited access to journals that they subscribe to, and have relatively little enthusiasm for pay-per-use models for electronic access. There is little empirical guidance at this time for publishers to learn how different forms of e-journal dissemination will amplify, synergize with, or erode their revenues.

The scholarly societies are possible loci of change in the systems of scholarly communication. The American Mathematical Society and the Association for Computing Machinery are both exploring electronic publication. These societies could experiment with posting electronic preprints of articles accepted for their p-journals as a form of member service. Since the membership fees in scholarly associations cover diverse "memberships services" as well as some journal subscriptions, the associations have some flexibility in shifting their investments, services and pricing.

In contrast, the commercial publishers only offer a set of journals and draw their revenues exclusively from direct subscriptions and related post-publishing income (such as permissions fees). Even so, we would predict more rapid rates of change in the overall scholarly communications systems if many associations and publishers were actively experimenting with electronic formats, rather than just a few.

Part of the dilemma is in encouraging prestigious scholars to take the risk of publishing in e-journals, or in electronic extensions of traditional p-journals to help enhance their legitimacy. The polymorphous model of the Journal of Artificial Intelligence Research offers some promise in the technologically savvy scientific associations, since they already publish their own p-journals. The other main shifts in the next two decades — perhaps more likely in many fields — is that scholars will share some of their preprints with colleagues via field-specific or departmental WWW servers (or whatever technologies follow after WWW).

These changes in scholarly communication could be accelerated if a critical mass of the highest status scholars in a given field were willing to publish their best work in electronic media. However, the highest status scientists have the least to gain in terms of personal visibility and prestige in such moves. And scholars whose status is just a bit lower are likely to publish in the same journals as the highest status scientists. And so on down the prestige hierarchies, until one reaches scientists who have trouble publishing in 1st and 2nd tier journals, and who have "less to lose." To the extent that scholarly communication takes place within a system of prestige that extends well beyond the immediate sub-disciplinary groupings, social change will be slower than if technical and economic conditions alone drove the scientific world.

Hess, Sproull, Kiesler and Walsh argue that networked discussion lists help improve the visibility and influence of scholars who are outside an inner circle within a field — ie. those who are in lower status institutions, institutions with weaker programs in a particular specialty, and those who are lower ranked. Electronic publication might also give these people greater visibility, if their e-journal articles were read by scholars in more prestigious positions or more central locations. Today, e- journals can be read worldwide by scholars and students with modest access to the Internet. But e-journals' isolation in a kind of ghostly netherworld of academic publishing doesn't help those who publish in them to be seen by prestigious and established scholars whose intellectual blood circulates in oral and paper networks.

Stevan Harnad (1995) offers a "subversive proposal" for ushering in an era in which e- journals replace p-journals:

> If from this day forward, everyone were to make available on the Net, in publicly accessible archives on the World Wide Web, the texts of all their current papers (and whichever past ones are still sitting on their word processors' disks) then the transition to the PostGutenberg Galaxy would happen virtually overnight.

Harnad's proposal to move scholars from one set of communication systems to another has much in common with many utopian proposals: there is no effective analysis of how to encourage diverse scholars make a workable transition. In practice, scholars will become interested in e-journals at varying rates. Today, a scholar who is facing a choice between publishing in a p-journal and publishing in an e-journal (other than JAIR) faces a choice between legitimate (but perhaps slow) publication, and more rapid publication in e-journals that are viewed as of lesser quality (or even not serious journals). The e-journal may promise world-wide accessibility. But the scholar who wants to be read by his or her colleagues is more concerned that the article be seen by valued peers than that it be seen by a possibly larger but much less influential group of readers. Today, p-journals are better able to promise appropriate readership than are e-journals, with a few exceptions.

The scholar who selects a journal to submit an article to for possible publication cannot wave a joystick and enact Harnad's subversive proposal. If the scholar is in a field where paper journals reign supreme and electronic journals are fledgling operations, there is little incentive to try the e-journal unless the scholar has serious problems being published in higher quality p-journals.

Some of the key features of the scholarly communication system that e-journal enthusiasts must face if they wish to accelerate the pace at which e-journals become legitimate. These include finding ways to synergize with the paper world, because readers will often print out articles for subsequent careful reading even if they receive them electronically. In practical terms, it can entail using stealth strategies such as those pioneered by JAIR.

The e-journals that thrive are most likely to be those who editorial boards can design formats that are compatible with the p-journal world, while adding e-journal virtues, such as rapid dissemination of accepted articles and the possibility of elaborate and computationally rich appendices.

7

Information Labour Market

The information sector is a relatively new construct. It is composed of those jobs in which people record, process or communicate information as a large fraction of their work. These are diverse occupations, including managers, lawyers, accountants, realtors, stock brokers, and clerks of all kinds. People process information in important ways as part of any job — including truck drivers, trapeze artists, and machinists. The label "information work" is a concise way to characterize jobs where information is a key product of the job, or where the person is likely to spend a large fraction of each workweek communicating, reading, search for information, or handling paperwork in its various forms, including electronic transactions. The information work force differs significantly from the hi-tech work force. The hi-tech workforce is composed of people who work in a variety of jobs within hi-tech manufacturing firms.

These firms have over half of their work force in hi-tech occupations, such as engineers and biologists. But

30-40% of their work force can be composed of people in other occupations, such as secretaries, accountants, assemblers and truck drivers. In contrast with the hi-tech work force, the information work force is composed of a specific set of occupations. The information work force gives us a complementary, but larger window, through which to examine social change. Information processing jobs are playing a major role in today's economy. Several analysts have argued that information handling is not simply a feature of existing jobs, nor even a central element in a few jobs. Rather, they see it as a key dimension for characterizing labor markets and urban economies. Castells, for example, simply declares that information handling is a defining activity in new metropolitan formations. He dubs leading edge urban developments as "an informational city." Fishman labels post-suburban regions as "tech-noburbs."

Thus he indicates that their dependence on transportation and communication technologies undergirds their social and spatial forms. Knight follows Daniel Bell's characterization of post-industrial societies, and argues that knowledge work is a core activity in a transformed urban economy. These provocative theses are worthy of investigation. They provide an important alternative entry point to the study of the work force in advanc-ed economic areas than do the traditional trichotomy of agriculture, manufacturing, and services. Unfortunately, analysts who write about the primacy of information work usually treat it as a "social fact." They rarely examine the meanings of information work in new social formations. In contrast, Lyons argues persuasively that information work should be examined as a new problematic, and not be taken for granted. Zuboff goes further than Lyons. She argues that organizations with highly "informated" jobs require specially skilled workers who can challenge traditional managerial styles and whose skill is a novel resource for mangers to cherish. The "information sector" is a relatively new analytical category which we believe is worth exploring. The United States work force is composed of people in hundreds of occupations.

Every simple category scheme mixes diverse occupations and working conditions. The traditional economic sector scheme mixes field hands and agribusiness accountants (agriculture); welders, stock clerks, and industrial engineers (manufacturing); cab drivers, waitresses, and lawyers (services). Dist-inctions between union and non-union cut across occupations, and depend upon local circumstances. Similarly, the crude distinctions between information work and other kinds of work mixes diverse occupations, like postal clerks and lawyers. But this chapter goes beyond the usual accounts of information work by grouping information workers into five occupational strata which differ in the typical quality of their jobs. This chapter examines the composition of the information workforce with special attention to simple differences between better and worse jobs. We primarily use demographic data to examine the changing composition of dif-ferent strata in the information work force.

The Concept of an Information Economy

Social analysts characterize the major economic transformations of this era with two different rubrics:a posti-ndustrial society and an information society. Some analysts loosely mix these portraits, but they have different connotations. The service sector dominates in Bell's characterization of post-industrial economies. He argues that post-industrial societies also depend critically upon credentialed experts, especially "knowledge producers" such as scientists and engineers. But scientific and engineering occupations form only a small fraction of the jobs in even the most technologically advanced societies. The service sector is dominated by a variety of industries, from transportation to restaurants, from insurance and banking to utilities. These service industries are composed of two key kinds of jobs:

a) jobs where people provide direct service — such as bank tellers, waitresses, stock brokers, lawyers, security guards, bus drivers, insurance agents, etc.

b) jobs in the administrative core of these organizations — such clerks, accountants and office managers of various kinds as well as specialists in marketing, computers etc.

In contrast, the imagery of an information economy focuses upon occupations in which the processing of information is a central and time consuming activity. All jobs require that people process some information, even if only sensory information to know where they stand and where they are going. But some workers also provide information as a central element of the services they provide. These jobs include certain service jobs such as teaching, practicing law, research, etc. They also include core admin-istrative jobs such as clerks, accountants, and computer programmers, wherever they may be found — in agriculture, manufacturing or services. For example, Scott (1988:178) notes that over 35% of the United States' manufacturing work force is composed of white collar workers. And most of these are information workers such as engineers, inspectors, clerks, and accountants.

Timothy Luke and Stephen White (1985:31) argue that capitalism has entered a new phase, informational capitalism in which "data-intensive techniques, cybernetic knowledge, and electronic technologies" are the new strategic resources for corporate production. They point out that core information services have expanded (banking, insurance, telecommunications, mass media, advertising, education) In addition, managers of service, industrial, and agricultural firms have invested heavily in strategies to base production on information: banks invest in data processing and electronic funds transfer, manufacturing plants invest in automated inventory control and robotics; agricultural firms invest in computer-based farm management programs; and managers in all sectors invest in information systems to support basic accounting and cash flow management. Behind these strategies sit a variety of workers — from the specialists who design them to the wide variety of people who use them.

Marc Porat estimated that the information sector accounted for more employment than manufacturing or services by 1950, and that approximately 46% of the work force was employed in the information sector in 1970.

Most of the occupations in the information sector are white collar jobs. The terms "white collar" work force and "information work force" overlap substantially. But they are not identical. Much of the growth of the information sector in this century was driven by the same forces which drove the growth of white collar employment: the massive gains in productivity in agriculture and manufacturing; the rise of services; and (especially) the rise of large bureaucracies — public and private.

Four sector Aggregation of the United States Labour Force

Experienced Civilian Workforce

Year	Information Sector	Agriculture Sector	Industry Sector	Service Sector	Total
1860	480,604	3,364,230	3,065,024	1,375,525	8,285,383
1870	601,018	5,884,971	4,006,789	2,028,438	12,521,216
1880	1,131,415	7,606,590	4,386,409	4,281,970	17,406,384
1890	2,821,500	8,464,500	6,393,883	5,074,149	22,754,032
1900	3,732,371	10,293,179	7,814,652	7,318,947	29,159,149
1910	5,930,193	12,377,785	14,447,382	7,044,592	39,799,952
1920	8,016,054	14,718,742	14,492,300	8,061,342	45,288,438
1930	12,508,959	10,415,623	18,023,113	10,109,284	51,056,979
1940	13,337,958	8,233,624	19,928,422	12,082,376	53,582,380
1950	17,815,978	6,883,446	22,154,285	10,990,378	57,844,087
1960	28,478,317	4,068,511	23,597,364	11,661,326	67,805,518
1970	37,167,513	2,466,883	22,925,095	17,511,639	80,071,130
1980	44,650,721	2,012,157	21,558,824	27,595,297	95,816,999
1860	5.8%	40.6%	37.0%	16.6%	
1870	4.8%	47.0%	32.0%	16.2%	
1880	6.5%	43.7%	25.2%	24.6%	
1890	12.4%	37.2%	28.1%	22.3%	
1900	12.8%	35.3%	26.8%	25.1%	
1910	14.9%	31.1%	36.3%	17.7%	
1920	17.7%	32.5%	32.0%	17.8%	
1930	24.5%	20.4%	35.3%	19.8%	
1940	24.9%	15.4%	37.2%	22.5%	
1950	30.8%	11.9%	38.3%	19.0%	
1960	42.0%	6.0%	34.8%	17.2%	
1970	46.4%	3.1%	28.6%	21.9%	
]1980	46.6%	2.1%	22.5%	28.8%	

Even though the terms "information economy" and "information work" are becoming commonplace, they often are used loosely. We see three problems with these casual usages:

(a) Many authors talk about an "information age" or "information economy" as a social fact that can be taken for granted . These accounts usually draw upon Porat's pioneering analysis which segmented the United States' economy into four sectors. The national data used by Porat, and often repeated in other publications, aggregates workers across regions with widely disparate industrial mixes and misses any distinguishing regional characteristics. Employment in rural regions such as California's San Juaquin Valley, centers of smoke-stack industry such as Gary Indiana, and service centers such as Hartford Connecticut, are all combined. But some metropolitan economies are much more information intensive than others.

(b) Many analysts who examine the information economy focus on the best jobs - particularly professional, technical, and managerial jobs. Some of them ignore the poorer jobs, such as clerical work in its various forms. Or they treat poorer jobs as transitional occupations which may soon disappear. Or they argue that office automation will eliminate a large portion of the least skilled "entry level" jobs Are good jobs or bad jobs most prevalent in an information economy? Is the mix of jobs tilting toward a larger number of better jobs?

(c) Some authors assume there is a natural evolutionary sequence from agricultural to manufacturing to service economies, and that information economies are simply the fourth step in the sequences. Daniel Bell argued that agricultural economies naturally evolve into post-industrial (service) economies, and sees the information sector as part of the

> infrastructure for a post-industrial society. We do not assume there is a natural four stage evolutionary sequence from agricultural societies to information societies. Rather, we treat the information sector as an important economic sector which crosscuts the traditional three sectors and whose occupational structure may shed interesting light on work in modern society.

Many commentators confuse the social meanings of information work by confounding it with the use of some form of information technology, especially advanced computer systems. For example, Giuliano advanced a typical interpretation of "information work" and "information-age" offices when he examined the shift of office technologies from pen and paper through typewriters and mechanical devices through interactive computer-based systems available on every desk.

He argues that the social organization of office work is evolving through three stages (a) an informal "preindustrial" office; (b) a highly regimented "industrial" office; and (c) a flexible "information age" office in which computerized information systems are available on every desktop. There are major technological differences in his illustrations of these archetypical offices. His preindustrial office relies on telephones, paper, and organized files. His industrial office relies on batchrun computerized information systems, as well as paper and telephones. His information-age office relies on universal desktop computing linked to interactive databases. He characterizes the information-age office as one which

"exploits new technology to preserve the best aspects of the preindustrial office and avoid their failings.

At its best, it combines terminal-based work stations, a continuously updated data base, and communications, to attain high efficiency along with a return to people centered work rather than machine-centered work. In the information age office the machine is paced to the needs and abilities of the person who works with it...-The mechanization of office work is an essential element in the transformation of American society to one in which information work is the chief economic activity."

Giuliano's article illustrates the typical confusion of information work and specific technologies. All of his illustrations refer to offices which are exclusively devoted to information handling in some form. There is no substantive rationale for distinguishing any one of these office forms as "information age" offices. The label glamorizes the kind of office technology which Giuliano would like to see widespread — interactive computer systems linked to integrated data bases. As Porat's study of the information work force shows, the information work force was 17% of the national workforce by 1900, and it grew to 30% by 1950 — long before electronic computer systems were installed in offices.

We believe that these computer technologies can be very interesting and become indispensable. But the ways in which they transform work is still open to question and investigation. As Iacono and Kling observe, "Despite the dramatic improvements in office technologies over the past 100 years, career opportunities and working conditions for clerks have not similarly improved.

Although clerical tasks today require more skills in using a complex array of technologies, these skills are not reflected in status or pay. A new generation of integrated computer-based office systems will not automatically alter the pay, status, and careers of clerks without explicit attention. "While these issues of pay, status, and career lines are peripheral to understanding how the labor process and phenomenology of information work differs from other kinds of work, such as craft work, we return to them in the next section when we examine the occupational structure of the information work- force.

Shoshana Zuboff's *In the Age of the Smart Machine* is the most daunting and serious recent study which examines the labor processes and phenomenology of work with computer-based systems. She provides vivid and often brilliant descriptions of the phenomenology of work with special computer systems in specific work settings. Superficially, her account differs substantially from Giuliano's.

For example her illustrations portray work-places like his industrial age office as much less pleasant work-places than information age offices. But she makes similar errors to Giuliano by not carefully distinguishing between the phenomenology and labor process of computer-based work and informa-tion work more generally. Like Giuliano, Zuboff coins a special term ("informate") with broad informational connotations to describe some special aspects of work with computers.

Zuboff identifies abstraction as a special feature of computerization rather than as a generic feature of symbol systems, whether represented by cunei form on papyrus, quill pen marks on parchment, pencil marks on paper, or data displays on an elect-ronic screen. Moreover important kinds of information work do not always entail the use of abstract symbol systems.

1980 Employment in the United States Information Sector: by Occupation

Occupation	*Employment 1980 (000)*
Fully Professional	
accountants	1,076
physicians, dentists, and related practiti	803
teachers, college and university	564
lawyers and judges	558
life and physical scientists	309
social scientists	285
operations and systems researchers and ana	173
architects	92
Semiprofessional	
all other managers and administrators	6,621
teachers, except college and university	3,209
nurses, dietitians, and therapists	1,607
engineers	1,472
writers, artists, and entertainers	1,313
bank officers and financial managers	659
computer specialists	598
social and recreation workers	509
school administrator, college and elementa	435
official and administrators, public admini	433
health administrators	213
librarians, archivists, and curators	201
vocational and educational counselors	183
research worker	180
foresters and conservationists	67
all other professional and technical worke	62
Upper Level Sales and Supervisory	
blue-collar worker supervisors, n.e.c	1,754

engineering and science technicians	1,127
sales representatives, wholesale trade	935
sales managers, including retail trade	721
real estate agents and brokers	598
health technologists and technicians	588
insurance agents, brokers, and underwriter	543
personnel and labor relations workers	461
buyers and purchasing agents	460
sales representatives, manufacturing indus	434
clerical supervisors, n.e.c	245
insurance adjusters, examiners, and invest	179
stock and bond sales agents	137
advertising agents and sales workers	112
inspectors, except construction and public	111
officials of lodges, societies, and unions	108
credit and collection managers	69
Clerical	
secretaries	3,944
sales workers, n.o.m.	3,149
bookkeepers	1,942
all other clerical workers	1,899
cashiers	1,592
typists	1,043
office machine operators	959
receptionists	644
estimators and investigators, n.e.c	545
bank tellers	542
shipping and receiving clerks	515

statistical clerks	396
teacher aides, except school monitors	391
counter clerks, except food	358
file clerks	332
telephone operators	323
postal clerks	291
mail carriers, post office	247
expediters and production controllers	238
payroll and timekeeping clerks	237
hucksters and peddlers	181
mail handlers, except post office	168
billing clerks	165
library attendants and assistants	155
ticket, station, and express agents	144
newspaper carriers and vendors	112
dispatchers and starters, vehicle	105
messengers and office helpers	98
demonstrators	92
welfare service aides	89
enumerators and interviewers	87
collectors, bill and account	81
stenographers	66
Blue Collar	
checkers, examiners, and inspectors - manu	750
printing craft workers	415
telephone and line installers and repairer	390
inspectors	150
radio and television repairers	122

photographic process workers	90
data processing machine repairers	86
office machine repairers	82

A good deal of information work also entails interpersonal communication, often face to face, but sometimes mediated by telephone — between students and teachers, judges and defendants, clerks and organizational clients. Although it is difficult to find occupations in which participants do not rely on any symbol systems, workers vary in the extent to which their world is mediated by symbol systems rather than communicated by personal experience. Hotel concierges and realtors, for example, often work with a good deal of key information based on their personal knowledge of localities and provide it to clients verbally. In contrast, other information workers, such as stock brokers, are much more wrapped in a complex world of abstract symbols and systems of relationships between them (e.g., stock prices, trading volumes, market averages, interest rates, transaction costs).

Through the 1970s and even early 1980s, most stock brokers relied upon paper systems, telephones, and specialized information services such as Quotron. By the 1980s, most stock brokers gained access to more complex information systems which provide a wider array of data faster and which allow easier comparisons between data. They can also routinely monitor and trade in a wider variety of financial instruments and international markets, ranging from Eurodollars to the Japanese stock market. Information technologies have helped reshape the job of stock brokers. Their work may have been much simpler in the 1960s than in the 1990s. But their knowledge was anchored in complex symbolic systems, although it was based on paper. The routine dynamics of stock markets and their relationships to other markets, such as money and bond markets, have not substantially changed because of computer systems — except for the special phenomenon of program trading.

Zuboff views computerized work as a major transformation in labor processes which diminishes the importance of the physical body as an acting and knowing agent. But Zuboff glosses key similarities between information work and computer based work. She focuses on a small set of cases in which relatively low level paper plant operators and clerks were beginning to use computer-based systems that were thrust upon them. Her sensitive observations about the phenomenology of computerized work in these special settings can often apply just as well to many forms of information work.

Giuliano's and Zuboff's accounts of information work, information technology and work illustrate common arguments about the kinds of labor processes which undergird information work. We find both of these accounts suggestive, but also misleading because they confuse information work with special kinds of work which uses advanced computer-systems.

We will not examine the phenomenology of information work in more detail here. While a more careful investigation would be very useful, it would apply to information work wherever it is done and in whatever historical period: London England in the 1600s, and Irvine California in the 1990s. But it will not teach us about recent changes in the work and labor markets within the United States without important additional information about the distribution of jobs, occupations, and technologies in the region.

Changes in the Distribution of Information Occupations: Studies based on different units of analysis could shed special light on changes in a regional labor market — a study of changes in specific occupations within the region, a study of changes in information work at the firm level, and studies of the occupational mix in a specific labor market. We will focus on changes in the distribution of jobs within the information sector of the United States as a way to better understand the changing mix of good and bad jobs. This choice helps shed light on the structure of information labor markets by using the same kinds of data that protagonists of the information economy use. Our basic strategy in this chapter is very simple.

(a) We have adapted Porat's characterization of information workers and his list of information workers which he used for estimating the size of the information work force in the United States. We use a similar list of occupations to estimate the overall size of the informa-tion work force in the United States in 1980. These are aggregate estimates of employment.

(b) We are particularly concerned with the mix of good jobs and bad jobs in the information work force. Many analysts treat the information work force as relatively homogeneous. We have divided information jobs into five status strata — professional, semi-professional, supervisory and upper level sales personnel, clerks, and blue collar information workers. We examine the relative number of jobs in each of these strata. For example, are professional jobs, such as accountants and lawyers, the largest stratum of jobs in the information sector?

(c) We are also concerned with changes in the information sector over time. Is the information sector still growing in relative size? Is the mix of good jobs and bad jobs within the information sector changing over time? To answer these questions, we examine the information sector in the United States national economy level from 1900 to 1980.

No one has asked these questions about the character of jobs in the information economy so directly. Some answers appear implicit in key writing about the information labor force:

Stratification of Jobs in an Information Economy Optimistic themes of universal progress undergird most accounts of the information economy. However, few authors carefully explain how good jobs replace bad ones. Giuliano implies that jobs will be upskilled. In three diagrams that illustrate his article, he indicates that highly specialized accounting clerks will become "account managers" when work is electronically integrated through the use of advanced information systems. Giuliano's claim goes beyond the arguments about upskilling and deskilling since he implies that job holders take on new jobs — moving from narrow clerical jobs like "posting clerks" to much broader "account managers". In bureaucratic terms, these information oriented jobs have simply been reclassified.

We were originally critical of accounts of information work like Giuliano's which casually assumed that semi-professional jobs would replace clerical jobs.

During the twentieth century, there has been a white collar revolution in the United States. White collar workers shifted from about 18% of the work force in 1900 to about 48% in 1974. Manual work remained at 35-40% of the work force during these 75 years. And farm work declined from 38% of the work force in 1900 to 3% by 1974.

We were also critical of accounts which focussed on professionals and ignored clerks, since clerks are a major occupational group in the US. Clerks grew from 3% of the national work force in 1900 to 18% in 1974 - a 6 fold increase. In contrast, professionals grew from 4% of the work force in 1900 to 14% in 1974 - a growth factor of about of 3.5. Managers grew from 6% of the work force in 1900 to 10% in 1974 - a factor of about 1.6. In 1900, managers outnumbered clerks by two to one; in 1974, clerks outnumbered managers by 1.6 to 1. Clerical jobs formed about 25% of the white collar jobs by 1974. Information jobs are not the same as white collar jobs. But they are similar enough to suggest that clerks work could form 20-30% of the information work force.

There are at least five kinds of criteria for ranking jobs from better to worse. Economic criteria focus on pay, benefts, security, and career opportunities. Psychological criteria focus on feelings, such as challenge, autonomy, boredom, and filiation with coworkers. Sociological criteria focus on prestige and power. Health and safety criteria focus on routine exposure to toxic materials or dangerous situations. Situational criteria focus on idiosyncratic features of jobs such as fit with one's personal life, flexibility of schedules, and the time spent commut-ing to work. These characteristics are not fixed for all people in a specific occupation. Ranking of jobs by these criteria can depend on the specific practices of particular employers and the specific preferences of particular employees.

Particular jobs may be ranked at one extreme on one set of criteria, yet be mediocre or poor on other criteria. Some industries such as transportation and aerospace pay their workers more for comparable jobs than do banking and insurance. While we recognize these complexities, we sought a simple strategy for characterizing the quality of jobs and comparing them over time. Any classification scheme that places some occupations into a "better work" category and other occupations into a "worse work" category simplifies complex criteria by which people assess specific jobs.

We considered two different ways to characterize the quality of jobs. We reviewed economic criteria such as income, and social criteria such as status, autonomy and related working conditions. We could not locate adequately detailed income data for each of the occupations in the information work force for 1900 to 1980 at the Federal level. Therefore, we turned to social criteria for comparing the quality of jobs in the information sector.

We followed Porat's, list of jobs in the infor-mation labor force. We went beyond his seminal work by dividing the information sector occupations into five broad strata. We constructed four white collar occupational strata and one blue collar stratum. The white collar strata range from fully fledged profess-ions at one extreme to clerks at the other. They do not include all white collar jobs (e.g., dentists), since we are examining the information sector rather than white collar work. We used standard sociological categories for professions and semi-professions. In addition, we identified one occupational stratum between clerks and semi-professionals.

(a) *Professional occupations* includes the 8 most highly professionalized jobs in the United States in the information work force, including accountants, architects, lawyers, and physicians. The most highly developed professions have legal monopolies over legitimate practice and credentialing requirements. These are usually the most prestigious occupations, and many of these occupations pay relatively well — on average. Jobs within these occupations vary considerably along other criteria, such as stress.

(b) *Semi-professional occupations* includes 19 groups which have some professional standing, and are not fully fledged professions. They include computer specialists, engineers, managers, school administrators, social workers, and teachers. Semi-professional occupations are usually less prestigious and less well-paid, on average, than the full fledged professionals. But they are usually much more autonomous and prestigious than the occupations in the next lower stratum.

(c) *Supervisory and upper level sales occupations* constitute a category whose status lies between that of semi-professionals and that of clerks. It includes advertising agents, health technologists, insurance agents, office managers, purchasing agents, real estate agents, and stock brokers. This is a complex stratum which lies between the moderately presti-gious semi-professional occupations and the less prestigious, less autonomous and lower paid clerical occupations.

(d) *Clerical occupations* includes clerical jobs of all kinds (including cashiers and sales clerks-). We view clerical jobs as problematic because they usually pay poorly compared with other information jobs. Clerical jobs vary considerably in autonomy — from telephone operators to executive secretaries. But they are often fairly regimented. And they usually provide few opportunities for moving to much more autonomous or substantially better paying jobs.

(e) *Blue collar occupations* includes technicians who install or repair communications, printing, and other information processing equipment.

Optimistic and pessimistic theories about the quality of jobs in the information economy can be evaluated by examining how good jobs and bad jobs are actually distributed across the five strata of the information work force. For example, the most optimistic stories suggest that the proportion of professional jobs (good jobs) should be much larger than the proportion of jobs in any other stratum. Further, the relative number of poor quality jobs should decline from one stratum to the next. This story, which we call "professional dominance" can be illustrated graphically. We can compare the shape of the curve which characterizes the actual empirical distribution of the relative size of the strata with the profes-sional dominance curve. We refer to the graphs associated with a particular story about the relative size of the strata as a "theoretical distribution."

These theoretical distributions are static. Most stories of occupational change in the information labor force are dynamic; the mix of jobs changes over time. Consequently, we will examine the fit of theoretical distributions to empirical distributions over time. For example, no one argues that professional jobs dominated the information workforce in 1900. But many authors imply that they do today. Thus we can examine whether the empirical distribution of jobs in the information workforce has been moving towards professional dominance between 1900 and 1980.

(a) *professional jobs dominate* the information work force: Most information workers hold highly professionalized jobs like accountants, scientists and lawyers; a smaller group holds semi-professional jobs such as engineers and school teachers.

(b) *middle level jobs dominate* the information work force: Most information workers hold middle level jobs. We have portrayed the alternative where the most dominant middle level jobs are the sales and supervisory jobs. The other information occupations are less numerous than these occupations.

(c) *lower level jobs dominate* the information work force: Most information workers hold lower level clerical jobs. The higher level occupational strata employ relatively fewer people, inversely proportional to their status.

Thus, these theoretical distributions range from optimistic portraits of an information sector which is characterized by generally good (professional) jobs to a pessimistic portrait of the same sector characterized by predominantly poorer (clerical) jobs. These distributions are static, but some of the theories describe information work as the end point of important "trends" — that the current distribution of information occupations is moving toward one of these three distributions. In the next section we examine how well the data about employment fit these three theories.

Scale, Growth and Structure of the Information Work force: The information occupations mushroomed in size from 17% of the United States work- force in 1900 to over 50% in 1980. In this period, the United States moved from a dominantly agricultural economy to a services economy.

Size Occupational Strata

Within the United States Information Sector, 1980

	Number (000)	*Per cent of Information Workforce*
Occupational Stratum		
Professional	3,501	6.5
Semi-professional	17,762	33.2
Sales and Supervisory	9,044	16.9
Clerical	21,130	39.5
Blue Collar	2,085	3.9
Total		
Information Workforce:	53,522*	53.9
Total Workforce	99,303	

*The information work force total is larger than that reported in above table.

The percentage of workers in each stratum of the information work force at the Federal level between 1900 and 1980. Professional and semi-professional workers have composed a remarkably stable proportion of the information work force between 1900 and 1970: 4-6% and 25-29% respectively. Together, these professional strata formed a minority of the information workforce — between 30% and 33%. Blue collar information workers slowly declined from about 4% in 1900 to 3% in 1960.

Since 1900, clerks have been the largest strata of information workers. They rose from 32% of the information work force in 1900 to about 42% in 1920. Clerical employment grew at a slightly faster rate than overall employment in the information sector between 1920 and 1970, when it peaked at about 45%. Simultaneously, the higher level sales and supervisory stratum shrank from 31% to 19% of the information work force. These two lower white collar strata formed the majority of information workers, and the relative number of mid level jobs has declined significantly since 1900 while clerical jobs have risen.

There are signs of a different pattern of occupational growth and decline between 1970 and 1980. As in the previous 70 years, the number of information workers continued to increase in all five strata. However, the relative size of some strata shifted in small but noticeable ways. The proportion of highly professionalized and semi-professional workers rose to about 40% of the information workforce. Clerks declined somewhat in relative size to 42%, although they continued to grow as a proportion of the total work force. In addition, the strata of supervisors and higher level sales personnel continued to decline. And the blue collar strata continued to decline in relative size.

Overall, the information work force mushroomed in the last 80 years so by 1980 it composed over 50% of the work force. Its lower level white collar workers outnumber professional workers. But this distribution has been masked by the steady growth of information sector jobs in the highly professional and professional strata, as well as clerical jobs. The occupational stratum between clerks and semi-professionals — the supervisory and upper level sales workers — has steadily declined in relative size. In 1900 it was twice as large, in relative size, as it was in 1980.

Two lower strata — clerks and sales and supervisory workers — account for 55% of the jobs in the information sector. Semi-professionals also account for a major fraction of the jobs — about 33%. But there is a large depression in the distribution of jobs across the three strata. The number of sales and supervisory jobs is about half the size of the semi-professional stratum and less than half the size of the clerical stratum.

The relative size of the five occupational strata does not fit any of the three theoretical models which we discussed above — professional, middle or lower level jobs dominating in a monotonic pattern. This distribution comes as a surprise. We expected that either middle or clerical strata dominated the information work force. We did not have strong expectations about trends in the relative size of strata. We were astounded by the stability of the relative size of these strata within the inform-ation sector between 1900 and 1970. And we were particularly surprised by the steady and precipitous decline in relative size of the sales and supervisory stratum. The kinked occupational distributions provide interesting evidence for segmentation in information labor markets. We examine the segmented character of information labor markets in the next section.

The Segmentati-on of Information Labor Markets

In this section we argue that information labor markets are divided into four relatively impermeable segments:

(a) clerical work;

(b) supervisory and higher level sales jobs, and

(c) the two strata of professional jobs;

(d) blue collar jobs. Our thinking has been strongly influenced by dual labor market theorists, even though their emphasis has often been very different.

Dual labor market theorists have primarily focussed on the segmentation between jobs in the primary and secondary labor markets. Most information sector jobs are primary sector jobs. Dual labor market theorists often mention that jobs in the primary labor markets are also segmented, but they rarely examine segmentation in the primary sector. The key element of segmentation pat-terns in labor markets is that significant structural barriers inhibit people's mobility from one labor market to another - or, in our case, one occupational stratum to another.

Our arguments that the information labor markets are segmented are very simple. Most occupations in the professional and semi-professional strata are segmented primarily by special education and licensing requirements. All of the occupations which we have listed as professions require specialized college or post-graduate degrees. Some, professions, such as law and medicine, impose stringent professional licensing requirements.

Many of the semi-professions have similar barriers that inhibit people from "moving up" into them, although some of them do not require formal training or licensing. "Writers, artists, and entertainers" are perhaps the most intriguing occupations since theoretically anyone can write, paint or play. But managers and administrators account for the majority of semi-professional jobs in the United States' economy.

Our data reveal a less apparent structural barrier that seals many women into clerical careers. Women who wish to rise from clerical jobs to "something better" often lack the special education and credentials required for fully professional and semi-professional jobs. Management is the primary semi-professional occupation which does not require college credentialling. Historically managerial jobs have been male dominated, while many clerical specialties became female dominated by 1900. While managerial jobs have become more open to women in the last decade, they have remained male dominated. Some structural barriers still limit women's mobility from clerical jobs to managerial jobs.

The supervisory and higher level sales jobs are within reach for a larger number of clerks since they do not have significant educational and credentialing barriers. Some pay more than semi-professional jobs. But they have steadily declined in relative proportion from approximately equal to the number of clerical jobs in 1900 to be approximately one third the number of clerical jobs in 1980. Our argument is based on the relative number of slots for clerks in the next stratum: clerks who want to "move up" in the information sector will see a significantly smaller num-ber of jobs they can qualify for.

Several questions might weaken this numerical argument. We do not believe that the these counter-arguments have substantial force. But they are worth noting. We have no specific data about the occupational mobility of workers between these strata in 1900 or 1980 or at times in between. An argument that two occupational strata are segmented depends upon mobility data. Indirect evidence indicates that clerks often do not move into other kinds of careers. However, occupational mobility data would not reveal the num-ber of clerks who sought jobs in higher level information sector strata, but did not find them or were not recruited into them. Nor do we know the extent to which clerks would find the various jobs in the stratum attractive and would have sought them if they thought they were more readily available.

While sex discrimination in hiring has continued to impede women's access to certain professional and semi-professional jobs, their conceptions of attractive jobs also influences where they work. The higher strata jobs were probably not equally desirable to clerks at all times between 1900 and 1980. Clerical perceptions have almost certainly changed between 1900 and 1980. In the early 20th century, most clerks were men and they may have viewed sales jobs and supervisory jobs which require more initiative than many clerical jobs as acceptable, if not attractive. Traditional women, who dominated the clerical work force by the 1950s, may have found these higher level sales and supervi-sory jobs less attractive. However, the women's movement has influenced women's conceptions of acceptable careers in the last 15 years. As a consequence, we suspect that more women clerks would find these jobs attractive today than in 1960, if they could move into them. However, these "better jobs" have been declining precisely during the time that they could become a move up for many clerks.

While the information work force became more segmented, access to many information jobs has become more difficult. The educational and credentialing requirements for jobs at all strata in the information sector have generally tightened during this century.

College degrees were once the prerequisites for only the most specialized and technical or most professionalized occupations. Since World War II there has been a form of credential inflation; bachelors (and sometimes graduate) degrees have become commonplace requirements for many semi-professional jobs. Some employers are beginning to selectively hire people with college degrees into clerical jobs. Clerical work is probably the primary occupational opportunity for the majority of college educated women with degrees in the liberal arts who do not acquire professional or graduate degrees.

We found that the information sector continues to provide a majority of jobs in the United States work force. Information sector jobs vary widely in quality. We have characterized the quality of jobs by one dimension: location in the status hierarchy of occupations. This simplified conception captures important aspects of pay, status, autonomy and other working conditions. Relatively few information sector jobs are fully professional, and clerical jobs form the largest occupational stratum. When we examined the growth of the various strata between 1900 and 1980, we found that clerical jobs became more dominant, not less dominant.

We do not have direct data about actual occupational mobility. But our data suggest that the mobility of clerks is significantly limited by structural features of the information sector. The information sector is internally segmented, not just differentiated. The information sector will grow somewhat in overall importance, and clerical jobs will continue to grow in absolute and relative size.

It is easy to represent the information worker as a male professional such as an accountant, urban planner or engineer. This representation misleads. A female clerk is more accurate, although no stratum is so dominant that the other strata can be ignored. Contrary to the argument that the information work force is becoming professionalized through the use of information technologies, we have observed a steady growth in the relative size of the clerical stratum between 1900 and 1970. The growth of the semi-professional stratum has been less marked. It was relatively stable beween 1900 and 1970, compared with the other strata in the information sector, and it swelled dispropor-tionately between 1970 and 1980.

It is ironic that clerical jobs are still expanding when the educational level of women, as measured by the number of college degrees awarded, is at an all time high. Our own observations suggests that certain clerical jobs, like secretaries and bookkeepers, have usually become more varied as a byproduct of computer technologies and higher education. In fact, some managers report quite happily that they are now recruiting college educated women into clerical jobs which formerly drew only high school or junior college graduates. However, other clerical jobs, such as cashiers and counter clerks may remain relatively routinized, even when they have automated support through specialized point of sales terminals.

We had not expected to find the information sector structured like a dual labor market for such a long period of time. Because we focus on the information sector, our data do not tell us about key aspects of dual labor markets, such as the employment of skilled craftsmen or even of mobility between other sectors and the information sector. Moreover, we do not have the kind of income data to definitely answer key questions about "the declining middle class." These questions were outside the scope of this study. Even so, our data lend support for the declining middle thesis. Moreover, our data cast doubt on arguments that office workers are becoming more para-professionalized and professionalized. Based on our own field studies of computerization in white collar work, we believe that office work is becoming more skilled. Our data doesn't show substantially more job openings for office workers to enter semi-professional and profes-sional occupa-tions. These jobs normally require college degrees. Even the high skilled information jobs above the clerical stratum which do not require college degrees are in relatively short supply.

In a recent article, Robert Reich identifies three major segments of the United States labor force which parallel our own categories. His three segments account for about 75% of United States' employment: symbolic analysts (lawyers, investment bankers, management consultants, research scientists, academics, etc.); (b) providers of routine production services (clerks); and (c) providers of routine personal services (barbers, retail sales personnel, cab drivers). He argues that the United States' location in international markets makes the jobs of symbolic analysts relatively valuable and well paid. In contrast, providers of routine production services are often competing with low wage labor elsewhere in the world. However, providers of personal services have captive local markets, and can fare better than clerks. After all, one doesn't fly to Seoul just for a haircut or a cab ride, even if it is cheap! But a publisher may well have a book typeset in South East Asia, and thus displace clerical jobs in the United States. Reich's symbolic analysts parallels our professional and semi-professional information workers. His loosely argued thesis suggests an important dyna-mism which may reinforce the dual structure of information labor markets. It certainly merits further investigation.

We have not addressed the question whether massive technological change, particularly computerization and the use of advanced telecommunications systems, will alter the structure of the information occupations. Some economists predict major declines in the size of the clerical work force. But these projections rest on studies of efficiency gains on narrowly defined tasks and simple assumptions about the substitution of capital for labor.

As the information sector expanded, it took on many characteristics of the overall economy: jobs that vary significantly in terms of pay, status, and power. Moreover, its internal divisions reflect patterns of segmentation that have developed elsewhere in the society. Overall, the information sector has become sufficiently large that is not an alterna-tive to the dominant social order — it simply reproduces many of its features.

8

Information Policy Strategies

The global dimension of the Net requires new approaches to formulating the policy infrastructures needed to achieve the full potential of the Net. Commerce must invest in the development of these policy infrastructures and governments must support these new approaches; It is argued that in the absence of an effective balance between commercial needs and social requirements it will be difficult to achieve universal access. The Internet Law and Policy Forum is working on how such a balance might be devised.

The global information infrastructure creates a space the dimensions of which are nearly impossible to imagine. The combination of computers and related technologies with the dimensions of bandwidth provided by the multiple technologies of fiber optics, cellular, microwave and satellite transmission define an environment that will envelope our earth and, regardless of the risks of cultural degradation which are inherent in such a phenomenon, become an essential aspect of the lives of many humans, and certainly nearly all who live in urban environments. For those citizens of this planet, there is no question that accessing digital information will become an essential utility, equal or greater in value than the essential resources of harnessed power, water, and sanitary and civil living conditions. Information in electronic form, and the infrastructure on which that information is created and transported (and valued as an asset in the global electronic marketplace), is becoming a further asset by which the development of an economy will be evaluated.

Distinguished from the resources of power and water, however, information is not a natural resource. Instead, it finds its origin in the creative activities of humankind. In our writing, coding, processing, banking, artistic creating and other activities that produce intellectual capital, information (and its inherent value to facilitating economic development) has already evolved during this century as a resource for which its distribution is not governed by the pragmatics of its physical location, but by the policy structures and legal systems which define the rights of ownership, and the rights to protect ownership, in the information.

Information is, without question, an economic resource. In considering the challenges of achieving access to information, we must recognize and accept that the world's economies and nations have already positioned and waged enormous battles over the governing policy structures. The recent negotiations within the World Intellectual Property Organization (WIPO), both those which succeeded and which failed, illustrate the scale of the debates.

But the recent convergence of technologies which are fostering the vision of a global information infrastructure, and in particular the Internet, is distinguished by a characteristic that is often overlooked in the policy debates. The reality of this global space is that virtually all of its infrastructure is itself the private property funded by capitalism. In those nations in which the telecommunications infrastructure has been a responsibility of the state, we are witnessing its privatization at an amazing pace. In nations lacking significant communications infrastructure, we are seeing 'generation-skipping' in the investments--copper wiring is being bypassed for fiber, if not for cellular or satellite delivery. Such choices are occurring only upon the investment of private capital in the solutions--the investments must yield acceptable rates of return in order to induce the investment in the first instance.

The same is true for the software, networking tools, payment systems and other ?building blocks? which are becoming the required elements for conducting global electronic commerce—innovation is being spurred by the expectation of returns superior to investments that might be made in more traditional lines—manufacturing, construction or financial investments.

The situation presents us with an essential truth--a truth which must be taken into account throughout our consideration of the laws and ethics of cyberspace. It is a truth which the authors of the science fiction which first imagined cyberspace realized long ago. Quite simply, cyberspace does not exist, and the global electronic marketplace will not mature, if their function and operation will not produce acceptable profits to those who place their capital at risk. Moreover, taking account of the pace of development, investment and innovation which characterize the evolution of the global information infrastructure, the time periods in which the acceptability of those profits is to be measured are being compressed. Time, volume and velocity are simply being evaluated differently with respect to investments for cyberspace. The pressures for measurable performance and return are unparalleled--the impact of private sector capitalism cannot be under-estimated.

The demands are creating, across the infrastructure, an appetite for information which is becoming stronger with each failed investment in the technologies; as William Gates has observed, 'content is everything.' Criteria for the investments are being defined only in terms of the ability of the resulting products--whether hardware, infrastructure or software--to facilitate new revenue. But, regardless of the quality of the technology, what has become apparent is that the information, and its quality for entertainment, education, commerce, government or research, must be valued by the consumer or user if the technology is to be turned on and utilized.

Consequently, the information is becoming the economic currency—the global coin of the realm of cyberspace. And, as an asset with economic value, in digital form, information becomes even more defined by its monetary characteristics than by its values for education, research or development. The pressures of capitalism are thus also placing tension on how those creating the Internet and the tools for empowering digital access to information consider the complex, challenging demands for answers to the legal, ethical and policy frameworks that are as essential to the evolution of a global electronic marketplace as the technologies themselves. Compromised by the expectations for appropriate returns on investment, we have seen the first generation of the Internet blur the libertarian philosophy of its creators—'let there be no rules'—with the economic demands of the capitalists—'let there be no rules which impair the potential for adequate return'.

The resulting mantra has left much of the global community with the perception the Internet and its potential are endangered by a lawless attitude, without ethical values or social integrity, which is being accelerated by the forces of capitalism. Hence, many fear the Internet; governments, responding to fear, are investing enormous resources into the development of policy and regulatory structures which endeavor to eliminate those fears.

The objective of the exercise, in fact, is to endeavor to improve access by allowing cultural, political and social values to be considered and weighed in the process of achieving the best possible environment for accessing, for proper purposes, the greatest portion of the available information. In so doing, the predictability of the electronic space (and the risk of sanctions for non-compliance) is hoped to increase its desirability as a functioning resource to all.

But, contrary to perceptions, the defining forces of capitalism, and their pressures for results, are consistent with the calls of those seeking predictability within the global dimensions of cyberspace. The existence of clear, articulate standards, and in particular the existence of legal certainty regarding the consequences of using the technology for executing commercial transactions, is fundamentally essential to realizing a marketplace. This need for certainty began in the layers of standards which define the infrastructure itself—the rules which describe how data elements combine into packets, how networks connect, how data is transported and how applications interface.

Today, the debates around which, among others, this conference is convened, only begin to introduce us to the last layers—the legal and policy structures which will provide true inter-operability. But the need for these structures to be disciplined into predictable, certain rules is equally imperative. Without clarity throughout the full structure, the environment is dysfunctional. Without functionality, capital has no interest. This scenario, in fact, accelerates a different type of risk—the risk of marginalization. If we are to discuss pursuing universal access to digital information, we must commit to understanding the importance of a predictable legal infrastructure to facilitating that objective. Here is where the needs of a global community and the needs of capital investments converge. In nations and economies in which there is an absence of certainty and predictability in the legal consequences from the commercial use of the global information infrastructure, capital will not be attracted. In those circumstances, capital will move elsewhere, thus risking the marginalization of the subject economies even further.

The resources of the World Bank and other facilities committed to economic development will be insufficient. Time, volume and velocity will continue to have their expected consequences and drive capital toward the environments in which certainty and the potential for an adequate return on investment are most likely to be closely associated.

The global dimensions of the Net require us to consider new approaches to formulating the policy infrastructures that are required, including the legal system elements which, despite diversities in cultural and legal structures, provide a sufficiently harmonious environment for predictability to exist without regard to national sovereignties. This should not be the sole responsibility of governments and inter-governmental organizations, although they possess (and are demonstrating) the competence to respond. For example, OECD, UNCTAD and UNCITRAL are already hard at work on projects which are responsive to the needs for consistent, foreseeable legal frameworks.

However, taking account of the potential appeal of increased returns on their investments, commerce (and the sources of capital) can realize significant benefit from investing in the development of the infrastructure of law and policy that can sustain, and facilitate, universal access. What is required to attract that investment? More than mere capital resources are necessary; as well, governments must be prepared to seriously consider the work product of any initiatives within the private sector and, as appropriate, to cooperate with those efforts. This strategy presents an entirely different paradigm than the traditional model which characterizes much of the law-making processes of the world.

Even in advanced democracies, the paramount function of government is to provide the venue for governance. Yet much of the rhetoric from governments regarding how the legal structures for the Internet will be designed calls for self-regulatory work products to be significant in the architecture. The expectations for industry leadership are surprisingly consistent among developed, western nations. But the questions remain: what invites private sector investment in law and policy development? what invites government to take that investment seriously?

Nearly a decade of experience with facilitating electronic commerce has provided us with some insights into the strategies that must be adopted. Successful standards development, whether for technology or for policy, requires the following key (but not inclusive) attributes. First, the issue being considered must arise from the need of the marketplace for the problem to be resolved--solutions must be market-driven. Second, there must be agility to the process.

The participants must commit resources sufficient to allow a timely, focused effort. Significant policy issues, if not resolved quickly, have the capacity to exhaust the human resources which are invested; timetables, administered with discipline, must be pursued. Third, those involved in the process must be both the relevant stakeholders and, as well, must have sufficient critical mass to assure that the resulting work product will acquire some level of market acceptance. Fourth, there must be sufficient resources committed--financial, time and human in nature—to reflect the seriousness of the parties to achieve a meaningful result. Finally, there must be defined, transparent processes to assure the integrity of the means by which the solutions have been achieved.

Process is tremendously important to the challenge of earning from governments a deferral of their inherent jurisdiction to regulate the integrity and operations of the marketplace. At the global level, if the objective is to produce work product which may be 'imported' into national or regional legal structures or market functions, the parties must commit to defining, publicizing and adhering to the steps by which experts are engaged, input received and support for the resulting output achieved. The legal and policy structures which will govern the marketplace for digital information assets will not be built as a single system; rather, it will be constructed from 'building blocks' which must, in turn, be assembled into systems that align to the cultural, economic and ethical dimensions of the varying marketplaces in which electronic commerce will be conducted.

Accordingly, experience suggests that governments will have tremendous curiosity in the process by which self-regulatory solutions have evolved. Critical is to evaluate the need for, and fully embrace the opportunity for, government review and input of the work. The Net demands new models of conduct; our experiences, even to this 'early' date, suggest that the formal structures will simply not keep pace. But governments and commerce find a mutuality in their desire to achieve progress; what is required is to incorporate the attributes of successful process into authentic models that can allow governments to either defer to regulatory products developed within commerce (such as widely accepted model agreements, commercial codes of conduct, innovative dispute resolution mechanisms) or, as appropriate, to accept and enact into law model regulations which facilitate a harmonized environment. The resulting predictability thereby overcomes the reluctance of capital to invest in market growth and innovation.

But 'self-regulation' is not sufficient; governments will only defer and give respect to that 'self-regulation' which is effective in operation. Thus, clarity must be accompanied by a) the existence of well-defined standards for when behavior is unacceptable; b) articulate means by which to exercise due process for determining a violation; and c) meaningful sanctions to be imposed (and an agreed result as to what authority may impose those sanctions). For the private sector to effectively exercise its potential to invest in regulatory frameworks which accelerate predictability in the marketplace, the stakeholders must be prepared to commit to developing complete solutions within each incremental step of the process.

During 1996, a consortium of over 20 multi-national businesses invested in a pilot project to determine the potential for self-regulation. Operated under the name of the Internet Law & Policy Forum (ILPF), this project has endeavored to demonstrate the capacity of industry, in collaboration with government, to create a neutral venue in which the stakeholders of the Internet could convene and seek to develop harmonized solutions to the challenging legal and policy questions. Central to the strategy is to leverage private sector investment in order to produce work product which normalizes the marketplace and provides to economies entering the global marketplace of cyberspace the tools and resources to put in place appropriate legal and policy systems to give to private capital the necessary investment incentive.

Today, the sponsors of the Forum are evaluating the success of their exercise and making choices regarding the suitability of further investment; regardless of their decision, the needs of the global community, and the opportunities for private sector leadership, remain vital to how we design in the coming months the strategies for responding. The legal and policy structures required are essential to avoiding marginalization and, in that avoidance, we leverage capital to achieve progress toward universal access.

9

Privacy Protection in Cyberspace

Privacy is a powerful word with diverse connotations. Consider these examples:

— The teenager who doesn't want her parents listening to her phone calls with her new boyfriend, and criticizes them for violating her privacy.

— A family sitting down for dinner around 7:00 pm gets frequent phone calls from telemarketers who want to offer them great deals on car loans or prizes for visiting delightful vacation properties. The family members want "more privacy" during the few min utes that they spend together each evening, but are reluctant to turn off their phones because they may miss emergency calls.

— A young engineer is afraid to sign any political petitions, because she is afraid that her employer might learn of her signatures, not like her politics, and ruin her promising career.

— A talented accountant moves to Texas to live closer to his aging parents. He has serious trouble finding a new job due to medical reports that state he lost work from chronic backpain, and credit reports that inaccurately identify him as having mountain s of unpaid bills. He is never called for an interview and has trouble learning why he is ignored.

— A systems analyst who works for an office supply company is fired after he criticizes his supervisor via "private email." He thought that he had a right to share his private views with a co-worker. The analyst sees the company as an even worse place to work since the supervisor can read his subordinates email at will.

— A college student in a mid-western university is shocked to find an anonymous mailing to a public electronic bulletin board describing him as having served jail, time within a long note about the changing admissions standards. He is further mortified wh en some of his friends start avoiding him. The student wants to have the offending note promptly removed, and to confront his.

— A young systems analyst is upset that a company whose headquarters is nearby has been ineffectively storing toxic waste, thus pollutingpart of the local water supply. She skips lunch to join a peaceful demonstration in front of their headquarters, and no tices that several policemen are videotaping the demonstration. She doesn't want to become part of a police file and leaves the area embittered at the company. The analyst feels she was intimidated by the police.

Privacy has many connotations and has become a catch-phrase to signify diverse issues such as these. In their landmark article, "The Right to Privacy," Warren and

Brandeis characterized privacy as a person's "right to be let alone." This meaning ca tches some of what bothers the teenager, the family, and the young engineer. Privacy is an elastic term which has broader connotations. The family may also wonder, "Why are they always calling us, and how did they get our names and phone numbers?".

The accountant wonders whether potential employers believe something about him that he doesn't know. After all, he desires a job. He may soon want to know what information his prospective employers are using to screen their applicants and what is contain ed in his profile. He would like to see employers' criteria for hiring, (information which they treat as private). The accountant should know that they are using his medical insurance records and limit access to them. He would like to know that his credit report is grossly inaccurate and be able to correct it. The accountant is caught up in a large web of personal record keeping systems about which he has little knowledge and over which he has little control. For the accountant, privacy refers to gaining control over the ways that information about him is collected, verified, and passed on to other organizations.

The accused student may have served time in jail, but was looking forward to a new life that college would open for him. He would like to change his life, and also find out who is harassing him. The systems analyst would like to register her disgust at a company's dangerous handling of toxic wastes without developing a police record. Each of these examples illustrates some of the nuances of the term privacy.

The first selection, "Your Personal Information Has Gone Public" by Professor David F. Linowes, lists numerous additional cases in which people have been denied housing, insurance, and jobs. They were ignorant of the information about them that apartmen t owners, banks, insurers, and various employers were using to screen applicants and set prices. Linowes also reports some shocking cases in which people had immense trouble in having their records corrected when they were grossly inaccurate. The strength of the article is in the way he concisely identifies the meanings of threats to privacy through vivid examples of personal troubles. However, he doesn't examine how these social practices developed.

Linowes starts his article with the provocative claim, "Privacy invaders are all around us." But many of the people and organizations who are seeking information about specific individuals or sharing what they know may not see themselves as "privacy invaders." Parents who are interested in the well-being of their children, may see eavesdropping as a fair way to learn about a secret and potentially dangerous relationship. The banks that employ telemarketers are seeking good clients for their loans, so that they can earn money on their deposits, in order to pay their account-holders higher interests rate. A manufacturing firm may carefully pre-screen applicants for an accounting job with credit checks after having been embezzled by an employee who had huge debts to pay off, and so on.

The office supply supervisor may feel that the morale of his work groups is being undermined by a subordinate who continually criticizes him and makes fun of him to his co-workers. While some of these breaches of personal privacy could be obnoxious or harmful to one party, in most cases, they are not merely frivolous. What kinds of guidelines should we have to balance a person's privacy with other social goods, such as parental guidance, the ability to conduct business, and the ability to have citizens p articipate freely in political life? Before examining some of the debates about these issues, it helps to examine how North American societies developed their current privacy practices.

Record Keeping in Mobile Societies

People and groups in any society spend some effort in learning about and regulating each other's behavior. But the means differ, and social issues raised by different means also differ. In relatively small social units, such as families and villages, pe ople learn about each other's behavior through direct observation, inference, and gossip. And the forms of social control, introduced to help insure compliance with social expectations, can range from those that are gentle, to others that are harsh and e ven brutal.

A distinctive feature of villages and small towns is that many business relationships are based on personal knowledge. For example, store keepers and bankers know most of the people to whom they offer credit, and they also know the extent to which their customers are reliable. Yet even in small town societies, people sometimes find it necessary to deal with large and distant organizations, (e.g. government agencies such as tax collectors and the military).

During the last 100 years, there has been an astounding transformation in the ways that life in industrial societies is organized. New means of transportation, (trains, buses, cars, and airplanes) enabled people to become very mobile. In the early 19th ce ntury, most people who were born in the United States lived and died within 50 miles of their birthplaces. Today, in a highly mobile society, a huge fraction of the urban population moves from city to city, following better jobs and better places to live. Adolescents often leave their home towns to attend college, and may move even farther away for jobs. Further, over 130 metropolitan areas in the United States number over 250,000 in population. Even moving "across town" in one of these cities can bring a person into a new network of friends, employers, and service providers. This combination of mobility and urban development means that many people seek jobs, goods, and services from businesses whose proprietors and staff do not have much firsthand knowl edge about them.

The scale of businesses and the number of government agencies with huge clienteles have also increased in the last 100 years. In the 19th century few businesses had thousands of clients. An even smaller fraction of the public interacted frequently with t he larger businesses of the day. Similarly, government agencies were also smaller. Overall, most business was conducted through face to face (direct) relations. Only very specific government activities, such as taxing and drafting was carried out between people who didn't know each other at all. Craig Calhoun characterizes contemporary industrial societies as ones in which a significant fraction of people's important activities are carried out with the mediation of people whom they do not see and may not even know exist. Today, banks can readily extend credit to people who come from anywhere in the country. And they can do so with relative safety because of large-scale credit record systems that track the credit history of over 100,000,000 people . .The credit check brings together a credit-seeker and employees of the credit bureau who are related indirectly.

Other private firms, such as insurance companies and mail order companies, also extend services to tens of thousands of people whom local agents do not — and could not — personally know. In these transactions, judgments about insurability and credit worthiness are made via indirect social relationships, and are often mediated with computerized information systems that are operated by data brokers such as TRW Credit Data and the Medical Information Bureau. Furthermore, many new government agencies, responsible for accounting for the activities of millions of people, have been created in the 20th century: the Federal Bureau of Investigation, the Internal Revenue Service, the Social Security Administration, along with various sta te departments of motor vehicles, etc. The sheer scale of these services creates "environmental conditions" which provide incentives to organizations to use computerized record systems to help the maintenance of indirect social relationships become routi ne. However, organizations of a similar kind and size, such as banks or police agencies, differ in their aggressiveness in using new technologies and management practices.

The United States has developed a body of privacy law which gives people some explicit rights and protections in a few areas as well as restricting wiretapping and other invasive acts. . However, during the last 30 years, people have lost control over rec ords about them. Increasingly, courts have ruled that records about a person belong to an organization, and the person to whom they apply cannot restrict their use.

Consequently, inaccurate police records, medi cal records, employment histories, etc. can harm people without their explicit knowledge about why they are having trouble getting a job, a loan, etc.

Although a right to privacy is not set forth in the Bill of Rights, the United States Supreme Court ha s protected various privacy interests. The Court found sources for a right to privacy in the First, Third, Fourth, Fifth, Ninth, and Fourteenth Amendments to the Constitution. As our next selection, we include the Bill of Rights to the United States Constitution.

Many key social rights in the United States have been defended as privacy rights by the United States Supreme Court. Many of these privacy rights have little to do with computer systems, and are more linked to "a right to be left alone." Supreme Court Jus tices relied on privacy rights in Griswold v. Connecticut, 381 United States 479 which gave married couples the right to use to use birth control devices.

Prior to this ruling, some states banned the sale of birth control devices. The majority opi nion referred to "zones of privacy" created in the First, Third, Fourth, Fifth and Ninth Amendments. Similarly, Roe v. Wade, 410 United States 113 (1973), further extended the right of privacy "to encompass a woman's decision whether or not to terminate her pregnancy and justified its action by reference to the Fourteenth Amendment.

Value Conflicts in Controversies About Personal Record Systems and Privacy

Discussions of computerization and privacy are embroiled in a major set of controversies with big stakes.

On the one hand, some people fear that emerging computer-based information systems are helping to erode personal privacy. They would like to see cert ain kinds of record systems regulated or limited in scope.

Others fear that new ways of doing business rms and government agencies that have an interest in expanding their computerized information systems frequently argue hard against legal limits or substantial accountability to people about whom records are kept. They deny that problems exist, or they a rgue that the reported problems are exaggerated in importance.

The contention is that proposed regulations are either too vague or burdensome and that new regulations about information systems would do more harm than good. The proponents of unregulated c omputerization are wealthy, organized, and aligned with the anti-regulatory sentiments that have dominated United States Federal politics during the last 15 years. Consequently, they have effectively blocked many attempts to preserve personal privacy thro ugh regulation.

Managers and professionals in business organizations and public agencies characterize their searches for information about people in limited and pragmatic terms. They emphasize how they want to improve their rationality in making specific decisions, such as: whom to hire, to whom to extend a loan, to whom to rent an apartment, and whom to arrest. These searches for personal information are sometimes fair and sometimes invasive of their privacy from the viewpoint of individuals.

Some of the key policy debates about computerization and privacy of personal records reveal conflicting values, not just conflicting interests. There are at least five major value orientations which influence the terms of key debates (Kling, 1978). These values can also help us understand the social repercussions of computer-based surveillance technologies:

> *Private enterprise model:* The pre-eminent consideration is profitability of financial systems, with the highest social good being the profitability of both the firms providing and the firms utilizing the systems. Other social goods such as consumers' privacy or the desires of government agencies for data are secondary concerns.
>
> *Statist model*: The strength and efficiency of government institutions is the highest goal—government needs for access to personal data on citizens. The need for mechanisms to enforce citizens' obligations to the state will always prevail over other considerations.
>
> *Libertarian model:* Civil liberties, such as those specified by the United States Bill of Rights, are to be maximized in any social choice. Other social purposes such as profitability or welfare of the state would be secondary when they conflict with the prerogatives of the individual.
>
> *Neo-populist model:* The practices of public agencies and private enterprises should be easily intelligible to ordinary citizens and be responsive to their needs. Societal institutions should emphasize serving the "ordinary person."
>
> *Systems model:* Financial systems must be technically well organized, efficient, reliable, and aesthetically pleasing.

In different instances, policies and developments may

support, conflict with, or be independent of these five value models. Each of them, except the Systems model, has a large number of supporters and a long tradition of support within the US. Thus, compu ting developments that are congruent with any of these positions might be argued to be in "the public interest." Information entrepreneurialism is most directly aligned with the private enterprise value model for guiding social action. But, the informatio n capitalist approach can also support statist values in cases where public agencies use computerized information systems to model and explore alternative revenue-generating programs, to assess the effectiveness of social programs, or to track scofflaws t hrough networks of records systems. It is conceivable that information entrepreneurialism could support neo-populist consumer control, by constructing databases that report on the quality of commercial products and services, or by enhancing access to gove rnment records systems.

However, such uses are extremely rare, and are not accessible to the majority of people, who are not computer savvy. It is difficult to imagine that many new computerized systems would, on balance, automatically support libertarian values. In the last Part, for example, we examined how electronic mail, which is stored in computer systems, can lead to losses of privacy between correspondents. However enhanced privacy regulations reduce the extent to which computerized systems which support statist or private enterprise values further erode personal privacy in the United States.

The next six selections illustrate how debates about computerization and privacy are anchored in these value positions. The debates about computer file matching pit civil-libertarian against statist values. The debates about the proposed Clipper chip and government wiretapping pit statist values against libertarian and private enterprise values. And the debates about direct mail marketing pit private enterprise values against neo-populist values.

Computer File Matching

Government agencies are often charged with regulatory and policing activities on a new form and a new urgency with the advent of computer matching, a technique involving large data bases with unrelated purposes which are cross-checked for consistency. For example, a state's automobile registration records might be matched against tax records, looking for individuals who own expensive cars, but who declared only small incomes. Computer matching has been used to track down and withhold tax refunds from parents whose child support payments are in arrears; to ferret out young adult m ales who have failed to register for the draft; to detect ineligible welfare and/or food stamp recipients; and to locate former students with delinquent loan payments. Advocates of this approach, such as Richard Kusserow in our third selection, argue tha t it is simply a tool necessary to carry out institutional mandates (e.g. helping to insure that fathers pay child support). Critics rarely object to the specific ends to which matching has been put so far. They would like to see fathers pay their requ ired child support, to reduce welfare cheating, etc. At the same time, they see matching as Big Brother's encroachment on individual privacy. Today, the examples of computer matching are relatively benign, but there are no legal guarantees that the uses may not become more and more intrusive as we enter the 21st century.

Matching can assist in controlling various illegal activities, which is why the 1984 Deficit Reduction Act required all states to participate in matching programs. Although the precise number of matches that have been conducted is difficult to determine b ecause of the lack of a comprehensive reporting mechanism, the United States Congress' Office of Technology Assessment (OTA) testified that the number of computer matches nearly tripled between 1980 and 1983. OTA also conducted a survey on 20 percent of the federal-level computer matching programs that were carried out between 1980 and 1985. Even within that limited number of matching programs, agencies had exchanged 7 billion records. Moreover, estimates of the magnitude of computer matching benefits reported ranged from $4 to $54 for each $1 spent on a match.

The fourth selection, by John Shattuck, reviews various dangers of computer matching, among them the idea that matching involves a presumption of guilt. He also anticipates a criticism in a 1993 study by the United States General Accounting Office that the guidelines for overseeing matching efforts are much too weak and ineffective. Kusserow illustrates a "statist" value position and Shattuck's paper illustrates a civil libertarian argument.

This debate illustrates some of the ways that statist and libertarian advocates frame privacy issues. Since this debate was first published in 1984, the United States Congress passed the Computer Matching Privacy and Protection Act of 1988. The matching law permits government agencies to compare information from two or more sources to detect discrepancies, which are then examined to see if fraud or some other type of abuse has taken place. It also gives people affected by adverse findings in a matching p rocess a way to appeal, and requires that people be notified 30 days in advance of the cutoff of benefits.

Many of the issues raised in this debate also surface in other statist-libertarian debates over required identity cards to streamline healthcare services or to reduce the number of illegal immigrants in the United States.

Wiretapping, Encryption and the Clipper Chip

In the next selection, "Clipper Chip will Reinforce Privacy," Computer Scientist Dorothy Denning supports a new Digital Telephony law that the US Department of Justice and its Federal Bureau of Investigation proposed in 1992. This law would require teleco mmunications service providers to assist government agencies in tapping conversations and communications.

In the United States, the Omnibus Crime and Safe Streets Act of 1968 permits wiretapping only to investigate specific serious felonies if: the targe ted communications device is likely being used to facilitate the crime; normal investigative procedures have been used with past failure and future success is unlikely, or are too dangerous to use. Private taping phone conversations is a social taboo in t he United States However, Federal law, which applies to interstate phone calls, requires the consent of at least one party. But California and a few other states require that all parties consent to the private taping of an instate phone conversation. As an extreme example, a woman in New

York State was granted a divorce after her husband taped her phone conversations.

According to testimony by an official of the Federal Bureau of Investigation, fewer than 1,000 wiretaps were authorized at the local state and federal levels in the United States in 1992. FBI officials fear that new encryption devices will scramble telephone calls so effectively that a simple phone tap would not let them actually hear an intelligible voice. They have been eager to promote a specific family of encryption methods that would make it easy to unscramble encrypted phone calls when a wiretap was authorized through a court order. One of the most controversial portions of the FBI's proposal was the provision that certain Federal agencies would be designated to hold the keys fo r all conversations, even those that were not authorized for wiretapping.

In addition, new digital switching systems could mix diverse phone calls on the same line in such a way that it could be hard for a tap to isolate a single specific phone line and conversation. FBI officials argued that they needed new help from telephone companies and other telecommunications services to be able to effectively tap phones in the future. The FBI argued that telecommunications systems and networks are often used in the furtherance of criminal activities including organized crime, racketee ring, extortion, kidnapping, espionage, terrorism, or trafficking in illegal drugs and that the agency would be ineffective without an ability to conduct wiretaps. Denning's article articulates these issues from the viewpoint of the FBI and also explains some of the subtle technicalities that underlie this proposal and subsequent debates.

The proposed Digital Telephony law ignited a firestorm of controversy. Denning's previous article advocating her positions first appeared in *Communications of the ACM* along with eight critical commentaries and one sympathetic commentary by Willi am A. Bayse, an Assistant Director of the FBI's Technical Services Division.

The criticisms came primarily from two major value positions: civil libertarian and private enterprise. The next selection, by Marc Rotenberg (a lawyer who then directed CPSR's Washington office) illustrates a civil libertarian analysis. Rotenberg acknowledges the legitimacy of wiretapping in very special cases. But he is wary of the FBI's proposal because they haven't documented their case.

Some people noted that the FBI exaggerated the importance of wiretaps in investigating terrorism or kidnapping. In fact, the vast majority of wiretaps are used to investigate drug cases and organized crime. In an earlier publication, Rotenberg also observed that the FBI has not acknowledged its history of abusing wiretaps and harassing groups that sought progressive social change, especially in the 1950s and 1960s.

Some people who saw local police departments, as wel l as the FBI, infiltrate, disrupt and sometimes destroy legally constituted student and church-based organizations in the 1960s learned that police agencies at all levels of government have periodically undermined important democratic movements. In this v iew, giving effectively absolute powers to any police agency is likely to be a destructive gesture.

Direct Mail Marketing

There is a good chance that every day you receive some mail from banks, credit card firms, political groups, and/or mail order firms with whom you've never done any business. You might enjoy some of the unsolicited mail, find some of it to be a nuisance, or a waste of paper and postage. The average United States household receives between eight and nine pieces of promotional mail per week A confirmed mail order buyer may receive about 1,000 pieces a year.The privacy issues in direct mail d iffer from those of other practices in that the recipients of unwanted mail or phone calls are not deprived of jobs or important services. At worst, it can seem to be a manageable nuisance. One key issue is the question, "How did they get my name?"

In the next selection, "Privacy: How Much Data Do Direct Marketers Really Need?" Denison Hatch argues that direct mail marketers often collect much more personally sensitive data than they need. He argues that direct mail marketing firms should regulate t heir own behavior in a way which is respectful of potential customer's sense of comfort. Hatch is not a strong libertarian. He is, in fact, very critical of "the forces arrayed against us — the media, government, liberal do-gooders, as well as those in o ur own industry whose zeal for profits overwhelms their common sense and decency." Even so, Hatch argues that direct mailers should be sensitive to public concerns out of self-interest, and regulate their own behavior through specific "opt out" and fair information practices lest they be regulated.

Robert Posch, a vice president of legal affairs for Doubleday Book & Music Clubs Inc., argues vehemently against Hatch's concerns about the public's annoyance with some of the sloppy direct mail-phone marketing campaigns. He argues that the Mail Preferen ce Service (MPS), which has allowed about 3 million people to opt-out of receiving unsolicited direct mail, is primarily a public relations device. Writing in *Direct Marketing,* he argues: "Our opponents are competitive media (television, magazines, newspapers, etc.) which have the power to editorialize and create value perceptions in their product." Posch wants advertising mail to be treated as (commercial) free speech and to be given first amendment protections. He is a staunch advocate of privat e enterprise values, Posch's article also points to schisms in the business world — between mailing list services which facilitate direct mail-phone campaigns and print and television media that thrive on mass advertising.

Individual, Regulatory and Market Approaches for Balancing Personal Privacy With Other Social Values

The preceding selections illustrate how value commitments pervade the debates about computerization, privacy and social control. Even so, some people do not appreciate the value issues in these debates and do not find extensive personal record-keeping obj ectionable, arguing that "If you haven't done anything wrong, you have nothing to worry about". They think of record-keeping that fits the routine behavior of legitimate organizations; banks wanting to know credit histories, courts wanting to know prior criminal records etc.

Computer-based information systems can be used in a myriad of ways that fit organizational practices. Many of these practices are legitimate; some may be questionable; and some may even be illegal. Problems arise under a variety of circumstances, e.g., when the records about people are inaccurate and they are unfairly denied a loan, a job, or housing. In large-scale record systems (with millions of records) there are bound to be inaccuracies. But people have few rights to inspect records about themsel ves except for credit records. During the last 30 years, people have lost control over their records. Increasingly, courts have ruled that records about a person belong to an organization, and the person to whom they apply cannot restrict their use. Con sequently, inaccurate police records, medical records, employment histories, etc. can harm people without their explicit knowledge about why they are having unusual difficulties.

Many of the issues of data ownership are complex and controversial in themselves. For example, today there are major controversies about whether people who test positive for HIV should be able to keep that information completely private. In principle, t he question has nothing to do with computer systems. The controversy focuses in part on the public good served by being able to identify HIV carriers versus the concern that many people may avoid HIV testing if they cannot be assured of the privacy of th eir test results. In practice, the ability of organizations to share files electronically makes it more likely that personal information can pass across organizational, state, and national boundaries if it is shared at all.

This approach has a certain clarity, but it is misleading as well. First, almost everyone recognizes *some* point at which one's personal activities are nobody else's business. A person may wish only a specific party to know certain information: th e bank to know the purpose of a loan, the doctor to now the reasons for a visit, etc. Second, as the White House "enemies" list and the Japanese-American incarceration sadly show, it cannot be assumed that (legally obtained) information will always be us ed for legal and ethical purposes. Last, in a society where so many records are not under the control of individual citizens, and are unavailable for people to review for accuracy, people may be denied key social goods (like employment, housing, or credit) when inaccurate information about them is passed through the files of businesses and public agencies without audit.

Studies of existing records have revealed widespread inaccuracies and ambiguities, with some state criminal history systems having a majority of their records being inaccurate or incomplete. As Kenneth C. Laudon demonstrates, a person's arrest reco rd almost always remains "in the system", regardless of the disposition of the case (conviction, dismissal of charges, etc.). All too often, the records show no disposition whatsoever. And many employers are unwilling to hire applicants with an arrest record, no matter how the case against them was eventually resolved. Laudon also found that employers and apartment house owners, not just police, were major users of criminal history systems.

Many citizens have grown so accustomed to detailing their medical histories and handing over their social security numbers that they scarcely give the matter a second thought. Probably few of them realize the extent to which computerization provides a re cord of individual activities. An electronic trail of one's whereabouts is available via records of Electronic Funds Transfers (EFTs), airline reservation systems, rental car agencies, telephone calls, and credit card purchases.

These records may be used for salutary purposes in certain emergency situations. The movements of accused killer Ramon Salcido were reportedly traced by monitoring his ATM transactions. But in less extreme circumstances, certain aspects of one's life are arguably a private matte r.

Some video stores, for example, maintain an ongoing record of each customer's rentals. The sale of lists of videos rented by specific customers was protected by the Federal Video Privacy Protection Act in 1988, but stores can still sell lists that indicat e the category of videos that one rents (i.e. political thrillers, foreign movies, and perhaps much more refined categories). Given cheap long-term information storage, combined with interconnected data systems, it becomes progressively difficult for an yone to escape the record of activities that have long past. Diverse personal information is subject to compromise and abuse any time that an unauthorized party gains access to it. There is plenty of evidence that today's large-scale computer systems ar e not adequately secure.

A huge fraction of the literature about computerization, social control, and privacy refers to regulatory strategies for striking fair and sound balances between conflicts values and interests. These regulatory strategies vary widely from one country to another. For example, Sweden instituted a nation-wide Data Inspection Board in 1973 which licenses all data bases with significant personal records. In contrast with this highly centralized and bureaucratic approach, the United Sta tes regulates very few uses of personal data. And Hiramatsu notes that "Traditionally, the Japanese have not been very sensitive to the right of privacy."

The Fair Credit Reporting Act of 1970 (15 U.S.C. 1681) was the first comprehensive piece of Federal legislation to give consumers legal protections from difficulties of inaccurate credit records.

The Act requires credit bureaus to have "reasonable procedu res" for insuring the information that they collect and disseminate is accurate. It permits consumers to see any credit information that has been used to deny them a loan, and also contains provisions for consumers to contest inaccurate information or to fill in incomplete information.

But few people check their credit records with major data brokers like TRW until they have been denied a loan. It can then take precious months to straighten out inaccurate records or problems of mistaken identity. As a U. S. Government report aptly noted:

The fact that the Fair Credit Reporting Act will enable him to get errors in the record corrected can be small and bitter comfort to a traveler stranded in a strange city late at night because information about his credit-card account status w as inaccurately reported to an independent authorization service.

In 1974, United States Congress passed a Federal Privacy Act that embodies five major principles of fair information practices. While the Privacy Act applied only to Federal agencies, these principles have influenced many people's thinking about an approp riate structure for regulating other personal records systems:

1. There must be no secret personal data record keeping system.
2. There must be a way for individuals to discover what personal information is recorded and how it is used.

3. There must be a way for individuals to prevent information about themselves, obtained for one purpose, from being used or made available for other purposes without their consent.
4. There must be a way for individuals to correct or amend a record of information about themselves.
5. An organization creating, maintaining, using, or disseminating records of identifiable personal data must assure the reliability of the data for its intended use and must take reasonable precautions to prevent misuses of the data.

The Privacy Act gives individuals the right to access much of the personal information about them kept by federal agencies. The Privacy Act of 1974 also established a Privacy Protection Study Commission, which in 1977 issued a substantial report on its fi ndings and recommendations. Although computerization was not a focal point in the report, it is never far below the surface.

The Commission made 155 recommendations to develop "fair information practices". Many of these recommendations gave people the right to know what records are kept about them, to inspect records for accuracy, to correct (or contest) inaccuracies, to be in formed when records were transferred from one organization to another, etc. Less than a handful of these proposals were enacted into Federal Law.

In the last 15 years, numerous privacy laws have been introduced into various state legislatures and into the United States Congress. Most of these laws were effectively killed by representatives of the industries whose actions would have been constrained . Even so, a few laws have passed where organizations have had a strong interest in drawing customers with promises of confidentiality. The Right to Financial Privacy Act of 1988 and the Family Educational Right to Privacy Act enable the right of access and review by the data subject, require that data be accurate and place limitations on access by third parties. In addition, the Video Privacy Protection Act of 1988 prohibits disclosure of personal information in video rental records an d the Cable Communications Policy Act of 1984 regulates the disclosure of cable television subscriber records. But these few national laws are exceptions. Aside from the regulation of personal records maintained by Federal agencies, whole domains of rec ord keeping and record sharing, such as medical, employment, and insurance records are open to the preferences of the record keeping organizations. In discussing the regulations about telecommunications in the United States, Law Professor George Trubow ob serves:

> Subsequent to the break-up of our Bell System, a variety of entrepreneurs have begun to provide telecommunications services which vary from state to state and are virtually unregulated with respect to customer information practices. "Caller I .D." for instance, has been approved in some states without any opportunity for the caller to block disclosure of his phone number; other states have required this option. Additionally, the regional Bell companies which replaced the national Bell System have recently been permitted to develop and market data bases so they themselves can supply information about customers; previously, message-switching was the principal function of the "Baby Bells".

Analysts respond in diverse ways to this state of affairs. Private enterprise advocates like Robert Posch and statist advocates like Richard Kusserow are relatively happy and criticize additional legislation as hampering the competitiveness of business or the efficiency of government agencies. Civil libertarians like Marc Rotenberg and Management Professor H. Jeff Smith seek policies and laws which give people fair protections against record keeping and information sharing practices which har m people and which do not result in a compelling social good.

Civil libertarians face difficult dilemmas because new technologies can support new services or organizational practices which can reduce people's privacy. There are a few technologies, such as encryption, where more powerful methods can enhance the priva cy of communicants. But encryption is the rare example contrasting with the diverse technologies for collecting data, storing, manipulating, retrieving, portraying, and communicating it.

In the United States, privacy laws tend to be reactive — to be enacted after some explicit damage has been documented. For example, the Telephone Consumer Protection Act of 1991 was enacted after many people were sick and tired of receiving numerous pre recorded telephone solicitations when they were selected with autodialers and specialized databases. After a reporter obtained a list of videos rented by Robert Bork, a nominee for the United States Supreme Court in 1987, Congress passed the Video Privac y Protection Act in 1988. Some civil libertarians believe that passing privacy protection laws is insufficient, since the United States legal system now puts the burden of enforcement on individuals who have been harmed and who must seek redress through the courts. Historian David Flaherty concluded his study of privacy protections in the

Germany, Sweden, France, Canada and the United States with the observation that an agency to enforce privacy laws is a necessary part of an effect ive regulatory apparatus.

Some civil libertarians who have been long term observers of the dramas of computerization and weak public privacy protections in the United States and Canada have become discouraged with the possibility of creating an effective protective framework based on the current regulatory approaches. Kenneth Laudon develops a new approach in the next selection, "Markets and Privacy." He argues that giving people property rights in data about themselves and creating markets where people can receive fair compensati on for data about themselves is a viable alternative. Laudon provides a broad sketch of his approach and anchors it within interesting economic theories. The core issues are important: that personally sensitive data can have economic value, and that indiv iduals can make the tradeoffs between their preferences for privacy and the value of the data that they could sell. Unfortunately, Laudon doesn't examine the nitty gritty details. Could an insurance company reduce its rates by 20% to clients who are will ing to share all of their medical data? Would personal privacy be primarily a luxury, or would most data sell for so little that only those who don't care or are relatively poor would be very open? Even so, Laudon's market proposal sets a controversial ne w direction for structuring privacy protection and information access.

One other limitation of Laudon' approach is that people are now required to use certain documents such as drivers' licenses and Social Security Numbers (SSNs) as forms of identification. In the selection "What to do When they Ask for Your Social Security Number," Chris

Hibbert tells us about the history and controls over the use of the SSN. He tells us why our SSNs are poor identifiers. Hibbert takes an activist stance and encourages us to disclose our SSNs as infrequently as posisble. Hibbert is interest ed in making laws effective by encouraging people to know their rights and to argue for them when they are asked for personally sensitive data. His article builds on a deep American tradition of informed citizens actively protecting their rights.

Personal Record Systems

During the next decades we expect to see new streams of services whose technologies include computer components such as: on-line household-oriented medical diagnostic systems, vehicle identification and location systems, "smart cards" for shoppers, and so on. These information services attract customers, in part, by giving them a little more control over some part of their lives. But in collecting personally sensitive data and placing it in organizational matrices of information sharing arrangements whos e nature is not well understood by non-specialists, such systems also reduce many people's effective control over the use of information about themselves ("privacy"). What are the forces that underlie the expansion of organizations' gathering records abo ut people's lives?

One view is that bureaucracies have a natural appetite for information, since information represents a source of power. A second explanation is proposed by James B. Rule and his colleagues (1980) , who argue that much of the pressure for information gat hering stems from public demand that organizations make "fine-grained" discriminations in determining eligibility for goods and services. If, for example, all citizens were entitled to free health care, the need to collect information about insurance and employment would disappear. If all car drivers paid similar rates (rather than receiving "good driver discounts" and paying higher rates for many driving offenses) the demands for driver history informaticn would be reduced.

Mark Ackerman, Jonathan Allen and I examine a third view in the final selection, "Information Entrepreneurialism and the Information Technologies And the Continuing Vulnerability of Privacy." We link the adoption and use of new computer technologies for personal record systems to a set of social practices we refer to as *information entrepreneurialism*. Information entrepreneurial explanations focus on the active attempts of coalitions within organizations to organize production in such a way as t o take advantage of changes in society and information technology. The internal structure of North American organizations has been transformed in the late 20th century by the rise of professional managers who have been trained and rewarded to pursue mana gerial strategies that depend upon data-intensive analysis techniques, such as precision direct mail marketing and data-mining.

Information entrepreneurial practices are made efficacious by some of the major social transformations in industrialized society over the past century: the increasing mobility of populations, the growth of nationwide organizations, and the increasing imp ortance of indirect social relationships. Information entrepreneurial practices are also encouraged by the development of more cost-effective technologies for managing large-scale databases and making fast computations. Analysts organize, implement, and u tilize information systems to improve marketing, production, and operations as an organization shifts its managerial style to be more information entrepreneurial.

Information systems multiply, as cost accounting, production monitoring, and market survey p ractices become a key resource in advancing the organization's competitive edge. Only a small fraction of these information systems contain personally sensitive data. But across the United States, these can lead to hundreds, if not thousands, of new pers onal record systems created every year.

We argue that information entrepreneurialism relies on a set of skills that people are likely to learn by participating in specific social worlds including academic programs (such as MBA degree programs) and professional associations.

We examined some p opular MBA texts about information systems, and found that their discussions of privacy issues were relatively superficial. Schooling is, however, just one stage in learning and refining a new worldview for many of the managers who seek to innovate. The business press publishes (and exaggerates) stories of computerization efforts that promise better markets and profits.

Magazines like *The Harvard Business Review* and *Business Week* publish stories about using information technology, including data systems with privacy dimensions, for competitive advantage. But they rarely highlight the privacy issues in their enthusiasm to excite managerial readers about new ways of conceiving of business opportunities.

In addition, professional associations h elp managers learn diverse approaches to their trades. However, some professions, (e.g. marketing, finance, and operations management) computerization strategies play an important role.

Professional associations in these fields offer talks, workshops, and publications for their members which also help popularize key aspects of information entrepreneurialism.

This chapter provides a provocative sketch of the social system that rewards informational entrepreneurship, as well as some of the ways that talented people learn the relevant skills and orientation.

Debates about computerization and fair information practices will not go away, even though they catch public attention intermittently. For a variety of "sensible" social reasons, organizations expand their computerized record systems and their use of dat aveillance techniques.

It is difficult to document cases of real harm, because there are few organizations collect such information systematically. Consequently, those who see people losing control, and organizations becoming less accountable, place a lo t of weight on the relatively small number of well-documented problems. But, we wonder, is this an appropriate state of affairs? What social costs are we incurring as we wait for problems to become visible or to mount up until regulation - however late becomes necessary.

In the meantime, computer professionals play key roles in expanding the variety and uses of personnel systems. But, given that many such systems raise important ethical issues, the question arises as to why some computer professionals often seem untroubled by their advocacy. Some may argue that they are unaware of any ethical repercussions. Others maintain that computer science is a technical discipline, unconnected with value questions. Still others say that "If I don't do it, somebody else will anyway ".

10

Ethical Issues of Infoage

The word "ethics" is derived from the Greek word ethos, and refers to a person's orientation towards life. The core issues of ethics include ways to foster a good society, and doing what is right (or just). A good society depends upon patterns of activit y characteristic of the society and the opportunities that it typically opens for its members. For example, many people were offended by South Africa's harsh restrictions on the live sof black people during the decades of Apartheid. Removing South Africa 's controls on racial segregation is one step in it's becoming a better society. Doing "what is right" is much more within the control of individuals. But people's social positions can "throw up" different kinds of opportunities for doing what is right (rather than doing what is simply expeditious or self-serving). Everyone faces periodic ethical choices where values conflict and where "the right thing" is not always immediately obvious.

People in specific occupations face some distinctive situations that people in other lines of work rarely or never face. For example, a surgeon is much more likely than a librarian or computer systems designer to face frequent situations in which other people whom he knows may be rapidly healed or injured (or even killed) by making choices about how to cut them with a sharp knife. In contrast, the librarian or computer scientist may be much more likely than the surgeon to face issues where they make inf ormation available that some potential readers may find enlightening, while others may find it offensive and try to censor it.

The work of information and computer professionals offers many routine opportunities to "do the right thing" when they design, develop, implement computerized systems, and facilitate their effective use. Some computer scientists argue that software develo pment is saturated with ethical choices. For example, Robert Collins, Kieth Miller, Bethany Spielman and Phillip Wherry identify five features of software, and the first two are particularly distinctive:

1. Serious software errors can remain after rigorous testing because of the logical complexity of software;
2. It is difficult to construct uniform software standards that could be subject to regulation and inspection;
3. Software affects an increasingly large number of people, due to the proliferation and logical malleability of computers;
4. Any group can provide software, since large startup costs are not necessary. This leads not only to a proliferation of entrepreneurs providing software, but also to nonsoftware businesses adding a software capability;

5. Unlike other public threats such as nuclear plants or toxic waste disposal, software's threats are dispersed, not centralized.

The inherent complexity of most software means that the relative effort of information and computer professionals to develop high quality, to invest in testing, and to track and check bugs have important ethical dimensions, especially in safety-critical systems. It is easiest to illustrate the importance of ethical choices with dramatic cases where people can be (or have been) hurt by poor choices. In fact, some of the literature about professional ethics relies upon well-known disaster cases to examine key arguments.

Some Bases for Assessing Ethical Actions

The question of "what principles" apply to assessing the rectitude of actions in professional practice go beyond the content of a professional society's code. After all, the professional committees that develop a new code of ethics need some principles to help shape their work. And a professional ethical code should go well beyond the laws of a specific jurisdiction. Simply asking whether an action is legal or illegal does not provide sufficient guidance for professionals. We expect, or at least hope, fo r more than the avoidance of illegal behavior from professionals whom we wish to trust — whether they are doctors, lawyers, accountants or computer specialists.

Some professionals will examine cases like those posed by Donn Parker and his colleagues with an informal sense of fairness or workplace pragmatism. They prefer to be honest in their dealings with their clients and co-workers, but they won't fight their supervisors and risk being branded as a troublemaker or even being fired. But some scientists and industrialists suggest that professionals can use more sophisticated informal criteria. For example, Gale Cutler, who directed research at the Whirlpool Corporation for 20 years, suggests that questions like these can help professionals resolve ethical dilemmas:

* Is it balanced? (Is it fair to all concerned? Will my decision disadvantage or perhaps even bring harm to anyone— my employer, colleagues, customers, suppliers, the community? Does it promote win-win relationships?
* Can I defend it? (If I had to justify my decision would I feel embarrassed or uncomfortable?"
* How will it make me feel about myself? (Will it make me feel proud? Would I feel good if my decision was published in the newspaper? Would I feel good if my family knew about it?)".

These additional questions can significantly expand a person's frame of reference to help see her possible actions from the viewpoints of people who can be affected by her choices, by her family and community (via the hypothetical newspaper story). But th ese questions are hardly foolproof.

Some situations, such as cancelling a failed project and laying off technical staff, don't allow options that will be good for all parties. In addition people often misperceive the concerns of other people, especially t hose whom they do not know very well or see as very different in social status.

Ethical philosophers have articulated more formal systematic frameworks for assessing the ethical appropriateness of different behavior. While there are over half-a-dozen major kinds of ethical theories in Western philosophy, three of them can be particul arly helpful for information and computer professionals: universalist theories (associated with the 19th century German philosopher Immanual Kant), consequentialist theories (associated with the 19th century Scottish philosophers James Stuart Mill and Jer emy Bentham), and theories of a just society (associated with the contemporary philosopher, John Rawls).

Universalist ethical theories hold that the inherent features of an action make it right or wrong.

> "the moral worth of an action cannot be dependent upon the outcome because these outcomes are so indefinite and uncertain at the time the decision to act is made; instead, the moral worth of an action had to depend upon the intentions of t he person making the decision. It is assumed that good intentions will normally result in beneficial outcomes. Personal intentions can be translated into personal duties because, if we truly wish the best for others, we will always act in certain ways to ensure beneficial results and those ways become duties incumbent on us rather than choices open to us. Our personal duties are universal .... The first duty of universalism is to treat others as ends and not as means. No action can be considered ri ght in accordance with personal duty if it disregards the ultimate worth of any other human being.

Consequentialist theories focus on the outcomes of actions rather than a person's intentions. One well-known formulation, called utilitarianism, emphasizes creating the maximum benefits for the largest number of people, while incurring the least amount of damages or harm.

> utility ... refers to our perception of the net benefits and costs associated with a given act. The utilitarian ideal can be summarized by the phrase "the greatest good for the greatest number". The primary way of meeting this criterion is b y performing a social cost/ benefit analysis and acting on it. All benefits and costs of a particular act are considered to the degree possible and summarized as the net sum of all benefits minus all costs. If the net result is positive, the act is mo rally acceptable.

Utilitarianism is very similar to systematic cost-benefit analyses practiced by actuaries, risk assessors, and engineers.

Theories of a just society examine the nature of social arrangements rather than on individual acts. Philosopher John Rawls developed the most famous version of the approach with a very sophisticated version of the Golden Rule ("do unto others ...) .

Rawls asks people to conceive of the ways of organizing social life that they would prefer from a very specific vantage point — one in which they know nothing about their own capabilities and potentialities. Rawls places people behind a "veil of ignora nce" about their actual social positions, and argues that "reasonable people" would prefer to choose a society in which is tolerant of people's rights and equitable in distributing goods and services.

Computer performance monitoring (CPM) system can help us better understand their potential role in shaping professional actions. Stephen Hawk sketched a utilitarian approaches to CPM systems in these terms:

> Business owners, employees, customers, and society in general may all benefit from CPM. The profits returned to business owners could be increased if CPM improved the efficiency and quality of work performed by monitored employees. Employees c ould potentially benefit if such profitability resulted in increased wages or employment stability. Customers could benefit if monitoring brought about improvements in service/product quality, or lower prices. Finally, society in general could benefit fro m an increased efficiency and effectiveness of its workforce. These benefits, of course, need to be weighed against the potential harms resulting from CPM usage. The literature clearly presumes that monitored employees bear the brunt of CPM's harms .... R esearch indicates that CPM causes stress and health problems, that it creates the potential for unfair performance evaluations, and that it is an invasion of privacy. Utilitarianism suggests that decisions surrounding CPM need to evaluate both the benefit s and harms and choose the option that results in the greatest net good.

Hawk argues that a universalist differs in the way that she would assess the a CPM because she

> places importance on the intrinsic worth of individuals, emphasizing the obligation of business to respect the right of privacy, the dignity and the autonomy of their employees. For this reason .... monitoring systems would be judged to be une thical to the extent that implementing them breached these obligations. Consider, for example, a CPM system used to report on minute to minute actions of an employee. Whether or not the benefits to the

> employer of such a system outweighed the costs to the employee, a (universalist) would reject the monitoring as morally objectionable if she concluded that it violates the employee's right of privacy, offends his dignity, or undermines his autonomy.

A Rawlsian would examine a CPM very differently. She would ask whether there is a way to structure the work with a CPM so that some of the parties gain advantage, but that none of the parties are disadvantaged. The monitored worker is most likely to be disadvantaged if close monitoring is added on top of an existing job. The Rawlsian professional might examine whether the monitoring might be structured so as not to induce significant stress, whether the job might be structured to relieve workers' stress through more frequent breaks, or whether the workers might be paid sufficiently more money to compensate for additional stress. CPM may be added to an existing job if one or more of these conditions is met, but not otherwise.

Each of these ethical theories can lead to a different conclusion about the ethical appropriateness of adding computerized performance monitoring to a specific workplace. In addition, these theories often lead to different ethical assessments of the actio ns described in the nine cases written by Donn Parker and his colleagues.

Codes of Professional Ethics and Conduct

Many professional organizations, the Association for Computing Machinery (ACM) included, have adopted codes of conduct for their members. "Codes of Professional Conduct," the second selection examines the rationale for a new ACM professional code. Soc iologist Ronald Anderson and his collaborators observe that many occupational associations adopted codes of ethics as a symbol that they were "really a profession." Unfortunately, these codes of ethics proved difficult to enforce.

As examples from earlier Sections suggest, computer specialists and other people in positions of responsibility sometimes don't follow "self evident" ethical guidelines. One set of controversies concerns the extent to which professional codes can influence the behavior of people who may not be oriented toward ethical behavior The role of professional codes in law and medicine can be instructive. They set guidelines for professionally specific behavior that are not simply part of "common sense." And while a small fraction of actual abuses by doctors and lawyers may be penalized by their professional societies, we feel more confident with these standards weakly enforced rather than with no codes or professional enforcement at all. Despite the controversy among computer specialists about the value of professional codes, the A CM's original 1972 Code of Professional Conduct has had a very limited reach. It provided for sanctions against offenders.

Moreover, it focuses on the conduct of individuals and d id not address the issues of organizational responsibility. Punishment and reward for a corporation is quite unlike that for individuals. And those individuals who make key organizational decisions may very well not even be information and computer prof essionals, let alone members of the ACM or a similar professional society.

Anderson and his colleagues acknowledge some of these shortcomings, and argue that such codes best serve educational roles in identifying important professional ideals. They may also sometimes help people make concrete professional choices.

The newer 1992 ACM is reproduced here as the third selection. Virtually none of the ACM's code is connected specifically with computing, except those portions that pertain to maintaining the privacy of data. Most can be derived from universalist ethical injunctions The American Society for Information Science (ASIS) has a shorter and simpler Code of Ethics for information scientists which specifies responsibilities to individuals and to society:

Responsibility to Individual Persons — Information professionals should:

* strive to make information available to individuals who need it
* strive both to ensure accuracy and not to infringe upon privacy or confidentiality in providing information about individuals
* protect each information user's and provider's right to privacy and confidentiality
* respect an information provider's proprietary rights

Responsibility to Society — Information professionals should:

* serve the legitimate information needs of a large and complex society while at the same time being mindful of individuals' rights
* resist efforts to censor publications

* play active roles in educating society to understand and appreciate the importance of information promoting equal opportunity for access to information

ASIS' code is less obvious than the ACM's code and it gives ASIS mmebers a more specific sense of direction. Career-minded professionals often find it difficult to make universal moral considerations paramount in the workplace. They are more likely to prefer a utilitarian calculus, since they can more readily justify occasional risks or ev en harm to some groups for the gains of others. But this common professional preference for utilitarian approaches is usually casual and sometimes self-serving.

A serious utilitarian analysis usually takes substantial thought and curiosity, since the an alyst must carefully assess the consequences of her actions upon all parties that are affected by an action. This requires a willingness to carefully examine potential harm and pain, as well as benign effects. In fact, progressive information and compute r professionals are arguing that all major computer applications should be subjected to informative social impact assessments before they are implemented on a large scale.

One interesting family of issues arises when commercial software products are oversold. It is easy for many computer specialists to blame an aggressive and fanciful marketing department or ad agency for exaggeration. But computer specialists who know the products best are often reluctant to help publicize their limitations or flaws. However, even principled computer specialists can have trouble insuring that their companies act with integrity.

An illustrative example concerns a major computer manufacturer that provided a FORTRAN compiler on a particular machine series, pseudonymed here as SUMMA. This FORTRAN was contracted and advertised to meet ANSI FORTRAN Standards. The programmer was assig ned to maintain SUMMA FORTRAN by implementing enhancements, repairing errors, and issuing memos about new developments.

Some of the error reports that she received from installations using SUMMA FORTRAN indicated subtle but important discrepancies between SUMMA FORTRAN and ANSI FORTRAN. FORTRAN programmers who believed that SUMMA FORTRAN was compatible with the ANSI standard wrote programs which did not appear to run properly. SUMMA's programmer prepared a variance report that she planned to send to all s ites which had adopted SUMMA FORTRAN. Her supervisor objected and argued that the firm could not acknowledge any discrepancy between SUMMA FORTRAN and ANSI FORTRAN since it was contractually obligated to provide an ANSI-compatible FORTRAN. She persisted, since she knew of the difficulties that the unexpected discrepancy between published specifications and actual behavior of SUMMA FORTRAN was causing in the field. After her supervisor threatened to fire her, she relented, and did not publish a report of t he discrepancy. But she was demoralized, and left the firm several months later.

The supervisor had little ethical justification for his actions; but he had the power of the paycheck to enforce his will. A strong support framework for a professional code of conduct might give some computer specialists, such as this programmer, a basis for insisting that their companies' products be fairly advertised, or that they be developed and tested with high quality tools and techniques. For example, this episode with SUMMA FORTRAN violates precepts 2.1 and 2.6 of the ACM's professional code. But the ACM provides no explicit support, such as counselling, legal advice or employment help, for members who believe that some of their company's practices are unethical. And any attempt to develop a strong support framework that could strengthen profe ssional standards, or provide protections for whistle blowers, will be embroiled in bitter controversy.

Unfortunately, professional societies for information and computer professionals may be incapable of effectively regulating their members' professional behavior if major computer firms do not encourage ethical behavior by their employees.

One of the distinctive features of the computing industry today is a relatively high level of technological innovation. Technologically innovative organizations often engender a form of smart, aggressive, and quick acting management that McAuley refers to as "mac ho management."

> displays of management competence which is characterized by such features as speed of decision, adeptness at "fire-fighting," displays of ability to control situations and people impersonally, and ability to manage crisis irrespective of human considerations — to act purely "for" the organization.... Kotter and Haskett found in organizations in which "macho" competencies were embedded a culture of "some arrogance, insularity ... supported by a value system that cares more about se lf-interest than about customers...." .

Intel's unwillingness to reveal computational flaws in the floating point performance of its highly advertised and very popular Pentium chip in 1994 seems to illustrate the ethical risks of macho management. According to management consultant Richard Pasc ale,

> Intel has no formal contention process but has a very contention-prone culture. It is driven by the personal style of Intel's president and CEO, Andy Grove, and that of his senior managers. Intel hɘs a 'gloves-off' way of interacting, which at times can be brutal, but it has helped Intel maintain its edge. It has a more direct and combative form of interchange than most companies would tolerate.

It is unlikely that such an aggressive culture would stimulate the kind of reflective approach that nurtures ethical sensitivity. And it would also be implausible for professional associations like the ACM or the Institute for Electrical and Electronic En gineers to discipline Intel in any significant way for virtually any business decision.

The Work of Ethical Analysis

Ethical analysis is very different from simple moralizing. It is a skill with both intellectual and emotional dimensions. It rests, in part, upon compassion for other people and an ability to see situations from the viewpoints of diverse parties who are e ffected by professional action. It also requires some refined analytical abilities to carry out systematic universalist, utilitarian, or Rawlsian analyses.

Robert Collins, Kieth Miller, Bethany Spielman and Phillip Wherry articulated a Rawlsian approach to developing application software. The method requires that the analyst identify all of the key participants, including technical staff, computer use rs, and so on. They also derived several principles from Rawls' theory of justice, including these three:

> *Least Advantaged*: Don't increase harm to the least advantaged. Software should not increase the degree of harm to those parties already most vulnerable to that kind of harm because of their lack of knowledge about software. Here degree (of harm) means (the) probability (of harm) x magnitude (of harm) and the harm can be financial or personal.
>
> *Risking Harm*: Don't risk increasing harm in already risky environments. Software designed for a low-threat context should not be used in a higher-threat context.
>
> *Publicity Test*: Use a publicity test for difficult cost-benefit trade-offs. Trade-offs between financial benefit to one party and personal (i.e., nonfinancial) harm to another party should be made on the basis of a cost-benefit ratio, that, if mad e public, would not outrage most members of the public. That is, make only those decisions that you can defend with honor before an informed public.

They applied these three principles in restructuring the design and operation of a hypothetical computerized system to support the operations in a hospital pharmacy. Part of their ethical analytical work involved examining the rights and responsibilities of different parties, and the repercussions of this ethical matrix for the effective design a nd operation of the computer system. Collins and his colleagues do not place all of this burden on the computer system designers. Medical staff who use the new information system as the hospital's managers also have substantial responsibilities in insurin g that the computer system is used effectively.

In many cases hospital information systems have been problematic in use, despite "good intentions" on the part of designers. For example, Ann Saetnan examined the use of a computer system that was supposed to make more efficient use of staff time a nd physical resources by automatically scheduling arrangements for operations in a Scandinavian hospital. She found that the scheduling algorithms did not effectively mesh with the work of doctors and nurses.

After some frustration, the staff used the com puter system simply to record schedules rather than to optimize them. Anthropologist Diane Forsythe examined the design practices of artificial intelligence experts who were designing diagnostic systems. She found that they interviewed doctor s away from the workplaces where they actually diagnosed patients. As a consequence, they generalized from their actual practices in ways that lead designers to conceptualize computer systems in unrealistic terms.

These systems design problems may seem to be misplaced in a discussion about ethical issues in professional work. But in the next selection, "Confronting Ethical Issues of Systems Design in a Web of Social Relationships" computer scientist Ina Wagner show s us how ethical issues can permeate key system design choices in a hospital. Wagner describes a study of surgical scheduling in a hospital that was supposed to avoid the kinds of scheduling system failures reported by Saetnan. Wagner observed that surg eons found ways to give their own patients priority, while sacrificing the overall quality of care in the hospital. She also found

Inherent in the clinic's operation calendar is a specific scheme of priorities, some of which are made explicit while others remain hidden. Some of these priorities mirror the internal hierarchy of specialties within the clinic, with heart surg ery ranking before all others. A second set of priorities derives from surgeons' ambitions to perform as many complicated operations as possible. As each surgery offers unique chances for learning (and for producing research papers), this ambition varies with the surgeon's professional biography. As a result, admission of patients is highly selective. In addition to professional preferences, there are other priorities, such as those which apply to emergency patients. Also, care values matter as in the case of old or particularly nervous patients or of patients who have to undergo a lengthy and sometimes painful preparation for surgery.

Wagner believes that a computerized scheduling system can promote more cooperation and effective use of re sources in the hospital:

> By improving access to information (e.g., on the current surgery plan, unscheduled time openings, changes of surgery teams and so forth) and by increasing the transparency of decisions, a system offers facilities for bridging organizational segmentation.... a system can (also) help to increase the degree of inclusivity and participation in decisions by giving an operation manager the appropriate tools to communicate events and to implicate members of the clinic when deciding (upon) the n ecessary ad hoc changes.

She identified four key design issues that had significant ethical content:

* Whether a person's use of working time should be known to others or private;
* How to negotiate the competing explicit and hidden priorities which guide decisions about the allocation of operation time;
* How to deal with the working culture of the "surgical team"—the time (and knowledge) of the different occupational groups involved in this team are not equally valued;
* Whether to strengthen the "automatic scheduling" capacity or the "cooperation-support" component of the system.

Wagner was particularly interested in designing automated personal calendars that could facilitate the planning of surgical operations, and notes:

Such calendars seem useful in complex organizations in which the availability of persons at certain times is not always known to those who make the planning decisions. The project team envisioned designing a tool that gives individuals (assistant surgeons, anesthesiologists and OP nurses) the opportunity to delete time, thereby indicating nonavailability for surgical operations.

At present, nurses (all of them women) and anesthesiologists have to be available within their working hours independent of individual time preferences and instantaneous commitments. To them the option of indicating temporal preferences could be attractive. Surgeons, (all of them men) on the other hand, have an interest in keeping parts of their individual time calendars private. This is in conflict with the need for temporal transparency of those who are responsible for the smooth running of the organization (in this case women).

In the course of her study, she struggled with four ethical issues:

— Identifying the legitimate participants in an intercultural dialogue;

— Admitting and handling conflict;

— How to implement "egalitarian values" in a hierarchical organization; and

— Thinking about the legitimacy of systems designers' own values and professional norms.

Collins and his colleagues were able to simply assume that all the hospital's staff would meet and talk openly with each other. Wagner, examining a real orga nization rather than a conveniently structured pedagogical case faced a much more vexing struggle:

> If in our case women's (nurses) voices are not heard, the resulting rules and regulations concerning "privacy versus transparency" will reflect a one-sided tendency to protect primarily the needs and interests of surgeons, hereby disregarding the organizational problems created when in an organization characterized by strong dependencies and frequent emergencies one group enjoys a high level of time autonomy (and privacy).

Wagner's observation about the relative invisibility of women's voices in systems' design echoes Lucy Suchman's (this volume) observations about the tendency of many male systems designers to undervalue the complexity and legitimacy of women's work. Wagn er knew that an automatic scheduling system would be more congruent with the way that work and power were organized in the hospital. However, she also knew that implementing such a system would require all parties involved to ignore existing conflicts o f perspectives and the ethical problems that she carefully identifies. Wagner's poignant study shows how ethical issues are inescapable in the design of important computerized information systems. She also shows us how Rawlsian scenarios that would bring together all participants to negotiate the nature of a just social order involves confronting organized power. Wagner's study powerfully melds the political and ethical dimensions of the work of systems designers in ordinary workplaces.

Ethical Action and Emerging Technologies

The pervasive computerization of various segments of society (education, military, business, communications) can have far-reaching impacts on people's lives rch project rather than another reflects a perception that the first is more valuable. Those who work in technical disciplines, although they may not directly decide which project is allocated to research and development groups, are at the very least ins truments of decisions made by others. Deferring to managerial authority is itself a normative decision.

There is, of course, a common belief that technology is somehow neutral or "value free". Yet, it seems highly artificial to separate the existence of various technologies from the uses to which they will almost certainly be put.

Technologies do vary in their range of likely applications. A high speed CPU, like the PowerPC, might be used in virtually any computer application. In contrast, a navigational system for a submarine torpedo or a diagnostic aid for scanning X-rays have such specialized uses that much less speculation is required. Even so, as we have seen with Ina Wagner's study, a consequentialist analysis requires considerable attention to social context and the social arrangements for actually using computer systems. For example, one cannot co nclude that all medical technologies (or, in her case, surgical scheduling systems) are necessarily good because they are used to improve people's health.

In the next selection, "Considering Privacy in the Development of Multimedia Communications," computer scientist Andrew Clement examines the way that a community of computer researchers engages with the social consequences of their work on multi-media communication systems. Clement uses the term Multi-media communication ser vices (MMCS) or "media spaces" to refer to a diverse set of technologies that connect people with audio, visual and/or computer links. You can imagine a office building complex with cameras, microphones, and speakers in every office, corridor, and meeting rooms connected in such a way that anyone can see people or listen to conversations or talk with anyone anywhere else in the office complex. These hardware networks are driven by software that is organized to help people find specific people, have small group discussions between people who are in different locations, and so on. These "electronic fishbowls" can enhance some forms of communication within groups, but they can also tighten then forms of organizational surveillance.

Media spaces have been a topic of research at major industrial computer science laboratories, including Bellcore, Xerox's Palo Alto Research Center (PARC), Xerox's European center (EuroPARC), and the joint DEC-Ollivetti Cambridge Research Laboratory. Thes e media spaces offer exciting technical challenges for talented systems designers who try to design them so that people can effectively navigate through them and effectively manage their communications. Clement also shows us how media spaces also open que stions about the nature of designs that give people a sense of effective privacy — such as knowing who is watching you and when and being able to shut an electronic door, as well as a physical door.

But the key focus of Clement's study goes well beyond the nature of communication and surveillance in these new media spaces. He is interested in the ways that information and computer scientists who develop social and technical architectures for these es oteric systems engage with the ethical issues that they raise. he observes considerable differences between different laboratories. The researchers at Xerox have been much more willing to characterize some of the privacy issues and treat them as topics of research than have Bellcore's researchers.

But Clement found two disturbing kinds of limitations in these engagements. First, the researchers have significant autonomy in their use of time, and significant abilities to redesign their media spaces so that it comfortably fits their workstyles. They are a universe away from Ron Edens' Electronic Banking System Inc. where a hawk-eyed supervisor discourages a squadron of regimented clerks from conversing and looking out the windows while they open envelopes and record financial transactions. While researchers can design electronic doors and have the option to close them, or design "I see you, you see me" visual reciprocity, organizations that buy media space technologies may be more interested in tightening an electronic cage than in se tting up electronic playpens. Clement noted that the researchers had trouble in systematically examining these alternative possibilities.

The second limitation is reflected in the eloquent comments of a research manager, who observes:

> We tend to have fairly short discussions in the hallway about the "dark side" [of computing implications], but quickly move past that to either the problem of the day or "We'll put this in and make it possible for that not to happen." ...
>
> There is a sort of psychology of ... innovation going on... We are all very uncertain about whether we can even get the short-term prototypes built, much less if the whole vision is right. So constantly we are boosting one another, saying "Oh yes , we can do it" and "We are doing the right thing", even though we all know we don't know whether we are doing the right thing .... But it is necessary to sustain the activities. That certainly works against anyone who tried to dwell on "how awful it co uld be" and "this could be the end of human freedom." [They] would not be welcome for very long, if they kept that up. No one would be able to get anything done, because we would all be so bummed out. ... That is the state of affairs, whether it is righ t or wrong. That is how it works.

In some of the laboratories, the researchers seem to be disarmingly uninterested in "the dark side" of their media spaces, and discuss them as issues that other organizations will have to address if they adopt these media space technologies. Clement notes ,

> All of these various factors .... tend to distance researchers and developers from active consideration of how the technologies may be used harmfully. Indeed, much of the direct experience with them will suggest that problems are relatively minor and can be dealt with. But it is one thing to experience personal discomfort and negotiate social/technical modifications with colleagues. It is quite another to take principled and potentially awkward stands on behalf of future users whose legitimate needs are vaguely defined and subject to a broad range of interpretations.

The unwillingness of leading industrial researchers to discuss these issues even within the technical communities can be awesome. Some of the computer scientists at Xerox PARC who were interested in discussing these issues in the technical community helpe d organize a conference wide panel session on "active badges" at the 1992 Conference on Computer Supported Cooperative Work. This scientific meeting attracts about 1000 computer and social scientists who study groupware, media spaces, and similar technologies.

One of the panel participants was the director of the DEC-Ollivetti Cambridge Research Laboratory. He simply refused to discuss any possible negative effects that could result from active badges, despite some direct questions about them from computer scientists in the audience. In contrast, other panel members were willing to examine diverse aspects of the use of active badges.

Overall, the social system of industrial development in the US does not encourage researchers and advanced developers to engage with the possible risks of their technologies that they can displace onto the shoulders of others, such as organizations that purchase systems based on their innovations. Clement closes his article for suggestions to help reform the social system of research so that social harms can be more readily anticipated and perhaps alleviated in technological designs.

11

Social Relationship in Network Environment

Electronic forums are springing up worldwide, and especially in North America. Millions of people are now corresponding through electronic newsgroups, bulletin boards, conferences, distribution lists and similar media. Somewhere, on the Internet, on a pr ivate service like America On line, or on an independent bulletin board, there at least one electronic forum that focusses on almost any topic that someone would want to talk (or write) about. And there many groups are organized for "casual chat" to help foster friendship, and sometim es even romance, between their participants. Enthusiasts for these forums argue that they are building new forms of community life. But other analysts observe that not every collection of people who happen to talk (or write) to each othe r form the sense of trust, mutual interest, and sustained commitments that automatically deserve to be labeled as communities.

This chapter examines some specific controversies about the kinds of social relations that people develop when they communicate via computer networks. The search for "a sense of community" has been an enduring theme in United States' culture. Ironically, t he technologies of freedom -- trains, cars, and airplanes; telephones, faxes, and computer networks -- have enabled us to be on the move, and to live, work, and do business with more people with whom we share very limited parts of our lives. Further, at a time when community life in North American cities is unravelling -- some people hope that people can meet and enrich their social lives at work and at home via computer networks.

This chapter also examines social relationships of people's physical lives -- not just their electronic images. It starts by examining social relationships in workplaces. Then it examines people's private lives -- their relationships within their pre-existing to wns, cities and metropolitan areas as they lobby their local governments for political change or search for romance online. It also examines how communities of authors and readers are shifting their relationships with electronic journals and digital libra ries.

Work Relationships and Electronic Communication

Many writers, including scholars, professionals and technical journalists, have speculated about the effects of new technologies on work life. Some speculate that electronic mail will eliminate organizational hierarchies, or at least reduce the barriers to communication between people at different levels of hierarchy in an organization and facilitate the formation of more flexible work groups (perhaps even "virtual" work groups).

Other speculations involve the extent and the conditions under which electronic communications will foster or undermine a sense of community in the workplace and elsewhere. Workers who are connected by electronic communications media may form "communitie s" that differ in substantial ways from other communities to which they may belong. Much of what has been written about networks at work has been concerned, in part, with community. A recurring theme of electronically-enhanced group cohesion is typified by Heintz, who claims that "the world of electronic science is smaller and more tightly knit."

Unfortunately, there are currently few empirical studies of changing forms of work that support these speculations. Technical journalists like Perry claim that "electronic mail has removed the barriers of time and place between engineers collabora ting on complex design projects." Aydin and Rice describe how networks bring together different groups in the workplace. There is some empirical evidence that computer nets help foster a sense of community among geographically or organizationally isolated professionals, such as special librarians and oceanographers

A substantial body of research has attempted to identify the unique characteristics of electronic media, and how new media use may be optimized. While much of this research is social-psychological in nature, a few researchers engage issues of organization al behavior. Kiesler, Siegel, and McGuire conducted controlled problem-solving experiments that compared computer-based communication with face-to face discussion. They found that the groups that used computer communication took longer to reach consensus, participated more equally, showed more willingness to arrive at conclusions that differed from their initial proposals, and displayed more "uninhibited verbal behavior" (colloquially known as "flaming"). So me of the effects that they observed have been attributed to the absence of non-verbal cues that are present in face-to-face discussion (body language, smiles or frowns, etc.) and even to some extent in telephone conversation (laughter, voice inflection, etc.).

The first selection, "Increasing Personal Connections," by Lee Sproull and Sara Kiesler set the stage for examining electronic mail (e-mail) and distribution lists in organizations. They argue that electronic mail is not simply a tool that replaces telep hones and paper memos -- it has distinctly different social properties. They argue that the use of e-mail enables people who are peripheral in organizations to become more visible. Lower level staff can communicate more readily to upper managers. People in branch offices or the field can communicate more readily with others in the home office and other branch offices. They argue that these electronic connections helps. democratize organizations by giving more visibility to people who are often out of sigh t or ignored by people in more central or powerful positions.

Sproull and Kiesler go beyond the normal focus on job specific communication, and also examine distribution lists where people can communicate about hobbies (the cinema list) or just hang out (the rowdies list). They argue that these formats for electronic communication also help people make connections and heightens the sense of social solidarity in organizations. These are important claims, especially for geographically dispersed organizatio ns or those that are experimenting with telecommuting.

But there is also the possibility that people's social relationships in networked offices may suffer in some ways. Research claims about e mail facilitating less inhibited behavior and flaming suggest that electronic groups may behave somewhat differently than face-to-face groups. Kezsbom, a technical journalist, sugge sts one possible down-side to networked worklife: "As the use of cross-functional, multi-disciplined project teams increases, the conflict that accompanies such team work will rise accordingly." And Zuboff reports the experiences of a large drug company where managers claimed that their electronic communications were being treated as policy statements, even when they wanted to make an informal observation or ad-hoc decisions.

"Gender and Democracy in Computer-mediated Communication," linguist Susan Herring examines the ways that men and women communicate in two different electronic discussion groups: LINGUIST -- devoted to the discussion of linguistics- related issues -- and Megabyte University (MBU), informally organized around the discussion of computers and writing. Herring uses a particular (idealized) conception of "democratic discourse" in which any participant can question any assertion, introduc e any assertion, and express their own attitudes, desires, and needs without being coerced into silence or compliance by other participants. She carefully examined discussions on these groups for the rates of participation by men and women. She went beyo nd counting the number of messages to examine the lengths of messages (the longest messages were written by men), and the style of interaction (supportive, critical, hostile). She also examined the ways in which people received rejoinders to the comments that they sent to the group, or their messages were lost in cyberspace without public acknowledgement. Herring summarizes her disturbing conclusions:

Despite the democratizing potential ... male and female academic professionals do not participate equally in academic CMC. Rather, a small male minority dominates the discourse both in terms of amount of talk, and rhetorically, through self- promotional and adversarial strategies.

Moreover, when women do attempt to participate on a more equal basis, they risk being actively censored by the reactions of men who either ignore them or attempt to delegitimize their contributions. Because of social conditioning that makes women uncomfortable with direct conflict, women tend to be more intimidated by these practices and to avoid participating as a result.... (the) conditions for a democratic discourse are not met: although the medium theo retically allows for everyone with access to a network to take part and to express their concerns and desires equally, a very large community of potential participants is effectively prevented by censorship, both overt and covert, from availing itself of this possibility.

Rather than being democratic, academic CMC is power-based and hierarchical. This state of affairs cannot however be attributed to the influence of computer communication technology; rather, it continues pre-existing patterns of hiera rchy and male dominance in academia more generally, and in society as a whole.

Herring's study is based on a very special sample of people (academics) and a special kind of forum: a discussion group. Perhaps other kinds of groups or other kinds of electronic forums more effectively facilitate democratic discussions. Social psycholog ist Giuseppe

Mantovani reviewed a broad body of systematic empirical research about the role of computer communication systems in enhancing democratic discussions between participants. Computer-mediated communication (CMC) tools, include both dist ance-spanning and time-synchronous systems, like teleconferencing, and distance- spanning and time-bridging asynchronous systems, like electronic mail (E-mail). These are diverse kinds of technologies, including those studied by Sproull and Kiesler and Markus in this Part , as well as those that support virtual offices. Mantovani carefully examines a position that has been most actively advanced by Sara Kiesler and Lee Sproull that "CMC is democratic because it supports participation in communicatio n in organizations in a way that is consistent with Western images of democracy."

The democratization thesis can be stated simply; but it has a number of complex dimensions that Sproull and Kiesler explore in their book Connections and in the selection from their book ("Increasing Personal Connections"). In Connections, Sproull and Kiesler summarize a rich body of research about face-to-face meetings that shows that meetings are often dominated by members who are highest in status, most verbally articulate, and/or speak the most. Lower status members, or those who are s hyer are less likely to influence the decisions made in meetings, even when they have important expertise. The democratization thesis mixes the moral value of democracy with the hope that more democratic organizations can more effectively draw upon the s kills and expertise of their employees.

Unfortunately, Mantovani uses an informal conception of democracy, without carefully identifying very different meanings of democracy, such as equal participation, one person-one vote, ability for minority groups to organize and argue for their interests, and so on. It is particularly important be clear about the differences between political democracy (in which the authority to govern derives from the consent of those who are governed) from conversational equality that is closer to the Habermassian conc eption of democracy explained by Herring. Democratic theorists like Pateman argue that effective political democracy at the national level is most likely in societies that have many arenas for people to experience conversational democracy and political democracy -- including their workplaces and their communities. But conversational democracy does not transform authority relationships into those of political democracy. For example, university students might enjoy conversational democracy o n a campus. But students usually play no significant role in selecting the faculty and administrators who exercise authority of over curricula and campus life.

Mantovani carefully examines a diverse body of research for evidence about the extent to which CMC use democratizes social interaction and social influence. Mantovani discusses a body of studies conducted by Tora Bikson and her colleagues that find that e-mail is effective in overcoming physical barriers, but not necessarily, social barriers. These technologies primarily enhance existing interaction patterns. He also draws upon Child and Loveridge's, studies undertaken in different Europ ean countries, that found that CMC is usually designed precisely to support ongoing hierarchical relations. Montavani concludes that whether or not CMC engenders democracy actually depends on the social context of CMC use, on the organizational history and on the rules determining CMC's application.

The next selection by M. Lynne Markus, "Finding a Happy Medium: Explaining the Negative Effects of Electronic Communication on Social Life at Work," gives us a concrete illustration of Montavani's abstract reference to "the social context of CMC use," "o rganizational history" and "the rules determining CMC's application." Her careful case study of the social effects of e-mail use examines communications between the staff at an insurance firm's headquarters (HCP). HCP's upper managers required their staf fs to rely upon e-mail, and it was the major medium for internal corporate communications at the time of her study. HCP's staff used e mail to speed communications and bring people closer together, But they also reported significant negative effects, such as feeling that HCP was a less personal place to work. Electronic mail was often used to avoid face to-face confrontation or unpleasant situations, and often in-office visitors were ignored while employees tended to the demands of messages on their computer terminals.

How should we understand the occurrence of these negative effects? Some analysts have argued that they are a byproduct of key characteristics of e-mail as a medium which reduces the intensity of important social cues, such as people's feelings. Markus challenges the "social cues filtered out" theory, and concludes that managers ascribe negative effects of electronic communications to "people's deliberately intended inappropriate behavior." The negative effects that she cited were primarily focused on depersonalization -- including employee feelings that the company was a less personal place to work, feelings of "invisibility," reduced feedback on job performance, and avoidance of personal contact. She believes that in some cases, these negative effects occur as ironic byproducts of people's attempts to avoid potential problems with system use. Markus examines how depersonalization may result from people's strategic behavior, such as using e-mail to send critical messages or forwarding messages to one's supervisor. This chapter has far reaching repercussions for analysts who conceptualize the consequences of new information technologies, such as advanced e-mail systems and groupware.

The studies by Herring and Markus raise important questions that counter our conventional notions of communication on computer networks.

In 1993, the New Yorker magazine published a famous cartoon of a dog at a keyboard who says, "On the Internet nobody knows if you're a dog." Visual cues, such as how one is dressed (if at all) or a person's physique, do not appear in written e-mail. But Herring tells us how writing style can help reveal a person's gender, in addition to obvious gendered naming co nventions, like John and Mary. And Markus shows us that people who know each other at work can effectively communicate many emotional nuances through written e-mail messages.

Of course, people can misinterpret e-mail, as they do verbal comments. Many peo ple hope that cyberspace can be "a place" where people develop more humane and democratic conversational relationships. And Kiesler and Sproull's studies suggest that electronic forums and e-mail can help people on the periphery of organizations and commu nities be more visible. But the evidence is beginning to mount that social relationships in electronic forums mirror many key aspects of face-to-face relationships.

Experiments with Community Life On-Line

Socializing and Romance On-Line

Although the first computer networks and conferencing systems supported communications between people who used them at work, the biggest growth now seems to be for people to use them outside of work -- for finding friends and lovers, pursuing hobbies, sca venging for investment tips, political organizing, and so on. As in other applications of computerized communication systems, these uses are often the subject of promotional articles. To be sure, many people have found new friendships on some of the nations 60,000 independent computerized bulletin boards, via information services like Compuserve, Prodigy and America On-line, or via complex networks like the Internet. In addition, these diverse services have helped spawn diverse discussion groups via Co mpuserve's forums, Usenet's newsgroups, and The Internet's LISTSERVs.

However, in the United States, communities seems to be deteriorating from a complex combination of causes. In the inner cities of big urban centers, many people fear street crime and stay off the streets at night. In the larger suburban and post-suburba n areas, many people hardly know their neighbors and "latch key" children often have little adult contact after school. An African proverb which says "that it takes a whole village to raise a child" refers to a rich community life with a sense of mutua l responsibility that is difficult to find in many new neighborhoods. Real estate developers can rapidly build a tract of 50 or even 3000 homes and give it a homey village like name, such as Deerfield. But communities that are based on people caring about and taking responsibility for the well-being of their members are harder to build. Some advocates believe that computer technology in concert with other efforts could play a role in rebuilding community life by improving communication, economic opportu nity, civic participation, and education.

Before examining some of these politically-oriented community networks, it's worth discussing some of the personal considerations that draw people to using computer networks to make personal connections. Without a broad understanding of what kinds of soc ial relationships people miss in their ordinary lives and seek on computer networks, it's too easy to overstate the value of high-minded civic and schoolish uses of computer networks.

For example, Usenet, a global replicated-BBS structure offers more than 3500 topic-oriented "newsgroups" on everything from PCs and Novell LANs to book reviews, music, pets, sex, and politics. How much of the Usenet communications is devoted to "high-minded topics" like science and technology, and how much is devoted to recr eational topics?

Usenet newsgroups include numerous topics, including discussions among cat lovers (rec.pets.cats), dog lovers (rec.pets.dogs), societal roles and relationships between men and women (soc.men and soc.women), as well as numerous specialized topics about com puter technologies, politics, world cultures, hobbies and so on. These newsgroups are organized into hierarchies: comp.* newsgroups (like comp.sys, intel) focus on computer topics, sci.* on scientific topics, soc.*, alt.* and misc.* include diverse socia l topics, and so on.

Usenet newsgroups constitute a small fraction of the world's electronic forums. But other kinds of forums also support interesting social relationships. Computerized BBSs (Bulletin Board Systems) that support "chat modes" sometimes foster special senses o f personal trust and intimacy. Though they are less personal than face-to-face communication, they can also reduce social distance. The French government's Minitel system has developed a set of "messageries" which enable people to develop friendships, in cluding romances, through simple terminals in their homes. The messageries have been popular tial controversy.

These systems are especially attractive to people who have trouble getting out of their homes to socialize ly the only, or even primary, users of these systems. But, for people with restricted social lives, electronic systems may provide truly important avenues to expand their social circles. "On-line" friendships may develop between people who never meet fac e-to-face (FTF) In the next selection, "They Call it Cyberlove," Margo Kaufman reports her experiences in meeting others via computer services.

Kaufman started out indifferent to computer networks until a friend, Jon, seems to have disappeared. She found that Jon had sim ply been living like a hermit to his "physical world friends" while he spent much of his days on-line.

Jon drew Margo into his electronic world, and she rapidly became fascinated by the nature of her conversations on America Online. She felt empowered by being able to send an electronic mail message to president. And she felt that "the lost art of conversation is thriving online.

Margo began to chat and play games nightly on her computer, she also found some irritating interactions such as being "hit upon" by some aggressive men. Fortunately, she found a way to click them out of her life.

But in the end, Margo found that she was behaving similarly to Jon by ignoring old friends. Unlike Jon, Margo was married and had some "real-life (RL)" social interactions at home. Throughout her essay, Kaufman remains a wry observer of the interplay of life on-line and off-line.

Lindsy Van Gelder's tale of "Alex" discusses the way in which some people have developed unusually intimate friendships on these electronic systems. Although the anonymity afforded by electronic communication can exhilarate and libe rate, it also raises new possibilities for abuse.

Van Gelder's tale serves as a reminder of this fact since "Alex" impersonated a disabled woman. Obviously, violations of trust are possible in many different arenas; however, the ease of computerized acc ess to a special group of people, along with interactive yet voiceless dialogue, certainly aided Alex in perpetuating his fraud.

Some readers may detect a slight moral ambiguity in this particular case, since Alex indisputably did some good as well as ha rm. Yet, not only were his intentions manipulative and largely self-serving; some of his victims had a strong sense of "identity rape" as well.

Community Building Through Computer Networking

Kaufman's and Van Gelder's articles help sensitize us to

some of the nuances of life on-line. And they set a more realistic stage for discussing community networking than do articles that examine only the joys of life on-line. Kaufman and Van Gelder's art icles can stimulate us to question who will be drawn to spend a lot of their time communicating through computer networks, and whether extensive networking will enhance or undermine the vestiges of existing communities.

Cyberspace symbolizes a new American frontier full of unexplored opportunities, that stimulate high levels of excitement as well as fears of chaotic semi-organized activity and even personal harm. New frontiers attract adventurers, speculators and even con artists. Taming a frontier is a kind of work that favors people who are bold and action-oriented rather than timid or reflective. Community has been a kind of question in the United States, as well as an answer.

Sociologist Claude Fischer not es that discussions of community in the United States are marked with unacknowledged tensions. This is a country inhabited by people with diverse religious and linguistic traditions. American have been traditionally mobile. And a deep ideology of individu alism makes community sound like an oppressive organization, as well as a romantically warm concept. These contradictions are brought forth, but not resolved in Howard Rheingold's book The Virtual Community: Homesteading on the Electronic Frontier.

There have been several community networking experiments, including high-profile systems in Cleveland (Ohio), Santa Monica (California), and Blacksburg (Virginia). The following description of the Blacksburg Electronic Village typifies the enthusiasm of the experimenters for the potential role of widely available computer networks or conferencing systems for enriching community life:

The Blacksburg Electronic Village is a project to link an entire town in Southwestern Virginia with a 21st century telecommunications infrastructure. This infrastructure will bring a useful set of information services and interactive communic ations facilities into the daily activities of citizens and businesses. The project will encourage and nurture the development of applications and of delivery mechanisms for services designed for everyday life.

The goal of the project is to enhance the qu ality of people's lives by electronically linking the residents of the community to each other, to worldwide networks, and to information resources in new and creative ways. The entire community of Blacksburg is being used as a real-life laboratory to de velop a prototype "residential street plan" for the country-wide "data superhighway" being discussed as a high priority on the national agenda. The project is being conducted so that its most successful aspects can rapidly be replicated in future electro nic villages in the state of Virginia and elsewhere in the United States.

The prototype in Blacksburg will exemplify four characteristics essential to a successful electronic village:

(1) including an entire community to achieve a "critical mass" of users,

(2) focusing on interactions between people rather than focusing on particular technologies,

(3) providing applications tailored for each type of user, and

(4) implementing the project on a timely basis, so that community networking becomes a fundamental consideration in the vision and planning of the nationwide networking infrastructure.

Because of the tremendous power it gives to the individual, community networking can have the same revolutionizing effect in residential life and ordinary businesses as widespread telephone service has had. The key to the success of the telep hone has been the concept of universal access. The foundation upon which the Blacksburg Electronic Village rests is to have a network connection available for every home, business, and classroom in the community. Furthermore, adequate network access equi pment must be available allow use of the network on a routine basis.

Ordinary computers can be used for data and some types of image transfer, and TVs, VCRs, and camcorders serve as video transfer devices for optional video capabilities. A high level of service coverage and participation for data access is as important in community networking as it is in the telephone system. Unless a "critical mass" of people possess and access their network connections regularly, they may choose other methods of comm unication in situations when, for example, an Electronic Mail message is the quickest and most efficient method.

Also, the more commonplace the facility, the more readily each user will share his or her knowledge about how to access a useful database sea rch facility or in mentioning the availability of the latest "hot" discussion group about a current event in the community.

"Yakety-Yak, Do Talk Back!: PEN, the Nation's First Publicly Funded Electronic Network, Makes a Difference in Santa Monica" Joan Van Tassel examines early experiences with PEN. Van Tassel describes how PEN's use met many of its fou nders' hopes that it would enhance political participation in Santa Monica. Even homeless people were able to use public access terminals to organize on their own behalf.

But not everyone was enthusiastic about PEN. Van Tassel mentions some aspects of PEN's use that undermined a sense of community:

> "netbozo takeovers (massive missives from a few residents who dominate the system), excessive flaming (no surprise to cyberspace denizens), and topic digression. Some PEN users, including several public officials, withdrew from PEN conferenc es because of what they perceived as vicious, unwarranted personal attacks from flamers."

She also quotes a Santa Monica resident who wrote:

> "The city probably spends $200,000 a year on PEN. There are 85,000 residents, 5,000 users, and 150 heavy users. Why should the taxpayer pay so some crazy wacko can write 'fuck you' to the council members when he goes off his meds?"

Not only is PEN heavily used by a tiny fraction of residents, but the men and woman who use PEN represented a distinctive segment of Santa Monica's residents who make more money, are more likely to be male, and are more likely to be college graduates. The y are also much more politically active than the typical Santa Monica resident. Van Tassel's article helps identify the complexities of community building on public access computer networks and the nuances of success and failure.

"Taboo, Consensus, and the Challenge of Democracy in an Electronic Forum" by Juliàn Dibbell is also a study of the complexities of building electronic communities. Superficially, the article is about an offensive cyber-rape that took place in a fantasy computer world. But Dibbell examines the ways that groups define their norms and forms of social control when some of their members are offended by some violation. It is easiest to be permissive and tolerant in both real life and in electronic forums when no one is offended or harmed by anyone else's behavior.

It is common for groups that meet in electronic forums to debate about the nature of behavior that participants find to be acceptable to them. For example, Usenet newsgroups periodically debate about the level of public personal criticism that is acceptab le, the kinds of message content that are appropriate for a specific forum, and so on. In particular work groups, there can be debates about the extent to which "personal electronic mail" can be shared with others.

Dibbell examines a group which as meeting in a MUD (Multi-User Dungeon) which was developed by Pavel Curtis, a Computer Scientist at Xerox's Palo Alto Research Center and made accessible over the Internet.

Participants (usually called players) have the appearance of being situated in an artificially-constructed place that also contains those other players who are connected at the same time. Players can communicate easily with each other in real time. This virtual gathering place has many of the social attributes of other places, and many of the usual social mechanisms operate there.

Although Dibbell and Curtis describe the use of MUDs for fantasy games, MUDs are also being explored as formats for on-line conferences and digital libraries. Dibbell's vivid article is a superb account of the ways that some participant s in a particular MUD (called LambdaMOO) observed a violation of their unstated norms, felt the violation as a real experience in their lives, and tried to articulate principles for punishing the violator (by expulsion/execution). Dibbell is specially se nsitive to the tenuous relationships between everyday life and the experiences of people in electronic forums. After describing how a character known as Mr. Bungle cyber-raped two other participants in LambdaMOO, he notes:

These particulars are far from simple, for the simple reason that every set of facts in virtual reality (or VR, as the locals abbreviate it) is shadowed by a second, complicating set: the ``real-life" fa cts. And while a certain tension invariably buzzes in the gap between the hard, prosaic RL facts and their more fluid, dreamy VR counterparts, the dissonance in the Bungle case is striking. No hideous clowns or trickster spirits appear in the RL version of the incident, no voodoo dolls or wizard guns, indeed no rape at all as any RL court of law has yet defined it.

The actors in the drama were university students for the most part, and they sat rather undramatically before computer screens the entire t ime, their only actions a spidery flitting of fingers across standard QWERTY keyboards. No bodies touched. Whatever physical interaction occurred consisted of a mingling of electronic signals sent from sites spread out between New York City and Sydney, A ustralia. Those signals met in LambdaMOO, certainly, just as the hideous clown and the living room party did, but what was LambdaMOO after all? Not an enchanted mansion or anything of the sort--just a middlingly complex database, maintained for experimen tal purposes inside a Xerox Corporation research computer in Palo Alto and open to public access via the Internet.

Even so, people, who manipulated characters in a database, identified with them, and began to struggle with their rules for creating a civil society for LambdaMOO's participants. One ironic part of the process was that, after substantial deliberations, La mbdaMOO's designer and operator imposed a form of democracy on its participants. This article is much less about sex in cyberspace than a haunting contribution to the debates about social relationships and democracy in electronic forums.

How Freely Should Information Flow in Computer Networks?

The fact that information can be used to tighten social control. But the control of information also raises important problems. Information control (censcrship), traditionally discussed in the context of pr int and broadcast media, has taken on an important new dimension in the age of the computer. Here the issue is freedom of people's abilities to send and receive information on computer networks. Questions about who controls information in electronic netw orks have not been resolved in any absolute sense.

Presently, there is a significant mobilization to draw people onto e-mail and computer conferencing systems to communicate "at work" and "after work." Most of these systems are privately owned, either by employers, or by firms which sell conferencing ser vices (ie., Prodigy, America On-Line, Compuserve). The operators of both kinds of systems claim the right to monitor and control communications content, and rely upon 18th century conceptions of private property to ground their claims. In addition, there is a movement to expand "civic nets" whose explicit aims are to foster lively discussions about local politics. While the operators of these systems are usually much more respectful of participants' privacy and freedom o f expression than are the operators of some of the private systems, there is no commonly accepted normative framework for these systems.

The shift from face to face, paper, and telephone to computer-mediated communications, makes people's communications more persistent, permeable, less controllable, and more traceable. The persistence of messages sometimes puzzles people. Electronic communication can appear to people as a transient conversational medium, even though the messages usually have the persistence of archived text. Electronic forums are often permeable. Messages stored in e-mail or conferencing systems can be read v erbatim unobtrusively. In fact, most reading is unobtrusive to the message sender (and is more like paper mail than face-to-face conversations or even phone calls).

People lose control over who may read ("overhear") their electronic conversation. Overheard conversations can be repeated, but listeners are often aware that they are learning hearsay rather than a verbatim account. Even taped phone messages can us ually be heard by only a few other people. In contrast, computerized messages can be copied verbatim and rapidly sent to hundreds or thousands of potential readers. Electronic messages are often more traceable than their paper or verbal counterpart s. Face to face conversations are transitory, and leave no trace of their existence for someone who walks into the conversational space after the discussants have left. In contrast, letters may be dated, and indicate to whom they were addressed. Phone cal ls may be identified by the phone numbers, dates, times, and duration of phone calls. (Cellular phones may be identify a party's location). Email messages may also be marked by their time, addressing, size, and so on.

The operator of an e-mail system or conferencing system has tremendous surveillance capabilities, and censoring capabilities, if they choose to exercise them. In practice, surveillance has been infrequent, but occasionally surprises participants and chill s important discussions.

Electronic mail and the records of conferences are often explicitly contested terrain. Today, firms are being encouraged by both the apostles of "virtual corporations" and the Federal government to develop and institutiona lize telecommuting. Email use has become routine at most large US corporations and many smaller ones. Some organizations have issued specific policies, but these vary considerably.

Some companies, such as Pacific Bell, Nordstrom's, Eastman Kodak and Unit ed Parcel Service, inform their staff that E-mail will be monitored because it is company property and it is in the corporate interest to do so. Other firms, including Hallmark Cards, Warner Brothers, Citibank and General Motors, have established polic ies that focus on employee privacy rights and better data security measures.

There are a few documented cases in which supervisors felt threatened by employee's criticisms via e-mail, and had them fired. Cappel summarizes two of the most visible cases:

> In the Epson case, Shoars, a former e-mail administrator at the company's Torrance, California site, raised objections when she discovered her boss was routinely reading messages which passed through a gateway between the company's internal e -mail system and its external MCI communications e-mail service. Shortly after, Shoars was terminated, when the company claimed she opened an MCI Mail account for her personal use. Shoars filed two suits over this issue: a $1 million wrongful terminati on suit and a $75 million class action lawsuit on behalf of herself and others at the site who claim that the company invaded their privacy by reading their e-mail messages. In January 1991, a California judge dismissed the lawsuits, ruling that the st ate's telephone wiretapping law (which the plaintiff had alleged was violated) had nothing to do with electronic mail....
>
> In the Nissan case, two employees, who were hired to set up and run an e-mail network between the company and its Infiniti dealers, were threatened with dismissal when their supervisor discovered by monitoring their e-mail that they allegedly ma de some disparaging remarks about her and the company. When the two employees filed a grievance stating that their privacy had been violated, one employee was allegedly fired and the other given the opportunity to resign. The case of these employees was also dismissed by a California court, with Nissan successfully arguing that since it owns the computer system it has the right to read anything on it.

Zuboff's report on a related case may dim unbridled enthusiasms and lead us to wonder about the conditions most likely to generate these transformations. When a group of about 130 professional women formed a private conference that threatened male manag ers, participation was discouraged by upper managers and many participants dropped out.

Should workers have significant rights to treat their electronic communications as private? Why shouldn't Nissan's argument that an e mail system is private property, and thus messages are Nissan's property, guide our social norms? After all, in other workplace contexts such as telephone call monitoring, the courts have previously upheld the right of an employer to mon itor where "a valid business reason" exists. Langdon Winner portrays this position that privileges private property in hauntingly stark terms:

For those who manage the systems of computerized work, the structures and processes offer a wonderfully effective means of control. Here is an electronic equivalent of Jeremy Bentham's Panopticon, the ingenious circular design that allowed th e guardians of a prison, hospital, or school to observe every inmate under totally panoptic scrutiny, the system is, of course, totally opaque. They are allowed to see only what the program allows. Closely watched and clocked, workers within the city of icons may find even fewer chances to express their individuality or participate in decisions than they did in the old-fashioned office or factory. When space is intangible, where do workers organize?

Increasingly, people are being encouraged (or channeled) into communicating via electronic mail at work rather than by phone or face to face by private firms and recently by the Federal government. It's hard to argue that t his shift would best serve the public good if it were to lead to more panoptic workplaces and a depletion of social capital. As with the on-line services and community networks, the most appropriate policies would be those that give employees significant freedoms to exercise free speech and rights of association in their electronic workplaces. In some cases, they may be working from home, and only their electronic images will pass through the disks at work.

Electronic communications systems can encourage the formation of diverse groups. But managers are likely to eradicate electronic groups that threaten their power, except in those special organizations -- like universities and R&D labs --where there are strong norms against censorship.

Universities, for example, usually try to maintain norms of openness, and are usually permissive in allowing information that is not illegal to be posted on publicly accessible bulletin boards. However, if a posting offends certain groups, people will cl amor to have it removed. Many political, religious, ethnic, and occupational jokes are offensive to members of those groups. The line between humor and libel, "fair humor" and cruelty is not finite.

In February 1988, the administration at Stanford University blocked access to an electronic bulletin board posting from Usenet by complaints about a racially insensitive joke that appeared on a Usenet newsgroup. Similar episodes have occurred at other universities hen people complain and then restoring them when others complain about censorship! At Stanford, the administrative action was highly selective, blocking access to the files containing the allegedly offensive jokes, but not interfering with an unmo derated joke forum, or with many other forums (including a few that allowed students to discuss their use of illegal drugs, or to exchange information about sexual techniques and nude beaches). In response, Stanford's Computer Science faculty voted to tre at Stanford's computer systems with the same kind of academic freedom as the university library and influenced the administration to restore the controversial newsgroup.

In October 1994 controversy erupted when the administration of Carnegie Mellon University (CMU) in Pittsburgh Pennsylvania attempted to ban about 80 sex-oriented Usenet newsgroups from campus computers, including the alt.sex.* hierarchy, rec.arts.erotic a and alt.binaries.pictures.erotica. CMU's administrators felt that Pennsylvania law and recent court rulings forbid them to knowingly distribute sexually explicit materials to minors. Many of CMU's students are under age 18, and the university administr ators wanted to obey the applicable laws. The announcement noted that CMU intended to support free speech, and that the only criteria for censoring computerized newsgroups "is that either the intended purpose for which it was established or its primary use (majority of the posts) makes it illegal for Computing Services to provide access to the bulletin board." The administrations' actions were immediately protested by students, faculty, and nationally visible groups, including the Ame rican Civil Liberties Union and the Electronic Frontier Foundation. How can anyone fault CMU's administrators for wanting to obey their State laws? The questions arise in interpreting the extent to which CMU is bound by their interpretation of Pennsylv ania State law. For example, the university library and bookstore are likely to contain erotic novels by famous authors such as Henry Miller, Anais Nin, and Erica Jong. CMU's administrators were not about to censor their library and bookstore. In addition , there are questions about the legal status of computerized bulletin boards.

At the core of the CMU dispute is a question that goes beyond the campus and could touch every media and entertainment company that wants to do business on the info highway: to what extent can the operators of interactive media be held resp onsible for the material that moves through their systems? Are they common carriers, like the phone companies, which must ignore the content of the messages? Are they like TV stations, whose broadcasts are monitored by the government for fairness and suitability? Or are they like bookstores, which the courts have ruled can't be expected to review the content of every title on their shelves? And what happens when that content hops over borders and lands in a different city -- or country -- whose la ws and community standards may differ?

These issues were hotly debated on the Usenet newsgroups comp.org.eff.talk, alt.comp.acad-freedom.talk, and alt.censorship. In the next selection, "Applying Library Intellectual Freedom Principles to Public and Academic Computers" Carl Kadie who moderat es alt.comp.acad-freedom.news characterizes eight additional cases where someone attempted to censor a newsgroup for its contents. Kadie examines each of these cases in light of specific academic freedom guidelines which have been articulated by the Amer ican Library Association. Kadie is a strong advocate of free speech and encourages the people and organizations who manage electronic forums not to censor messages and files which some people may find offensive. The counterpoint position argues that there are some materials, such as racist hate literature, that are so damaging, that bulletin board operators should have a right (or even a moral oblgation) to be able to remove.

Communication, Persuasion, and Influence in Scholarly Communities

The Internet, which is often viewed as a symbol and prototype for new data superhighways, was developed and refined in specific academic and closely related R&D communities. We now turn to some controversies about the ways that electronic media are changing communities of scholars. Even though a good deal of university research involves long hours of solitary work, research takes on a special meaning within the social worlds which encourage it, utilize it, and reward (or ignore) it.

Electronic publishing has attracted an interesting group of enthusiasts who view them as virtually inevitable. Richard Lanham argues that electronic publishing will erode the importance of the codex book (a collection of pages, bound between two c overs in a fixed sequence) as "the operating system" of the humanities. Lanham suggests that the digitization of textual, audio and visual communications will encourage reorganizations of knowledge via hypertext. Common storage representations, transmiss ion protocols and manipulation algorithms will enable a confluence of data not previously achievable with analog paradigms. In Lanham's view, this technological capability makes inevitable a future in which the reader is the author and where copyri ght law is irrelevant:

Texts are not fixed in print but projected on a phosphor screen in volatile form. They can be amended, emended, rewritten, reformatted, set in another typeface, all with a few keystrokes. The whole system of cultural authority we inherited f rom Renaissance Humanism thus evaporates, literally, at a stroke. The "Great Book," the authoritative text, was built on the fixity of print technology. That fixity no longer operates. The reader defined by print‹the engrossed admiration of the h umanist scholar reading Cicero‹now becomes quite another person. He can quarrel with the text, and not marginally, or next year in another book, but right now, integrally. The reader thus becomes an author. Author and authority are both transforme d.

Let us consider the dreariest textbook of all, the Freshman Composition Handbook. You all know them. Heavy. Shiny coated paper. Pyroxylin, peanut-butter-sandwich-proof cover. Imagine instead an online program available to everyone who teaches, and everyone who takes, the course. The apoplexy that comp handbooks always generate now finds more than marginal expression. Stupid examples are critiqued as such; better ones are found. Teachers contribute their experience on how the book works, or doesn't work, in action. The textbook, rather than fixed in an edition, is a continually changing, evolutionary document. It is fed by all the people who use it, and continually made and remade by them.

Lanham explores this exciting imagery of people communicating differently through electronic reading and writing as a lively alternative to the relatively static world of traditional printed books. Lanham doesn't examine how these electronic academic com munities will develop in practice. For example, imagine that you had an electronic copy of his article, and that you disagreed with some of his arguments. How could you communicate your disagreement to other people who also have his paper on-line? Would you have to post your commentaries in a centralized archive? Could you send them as messages throughout a network? The mechanics of making electronic communication matters as much in the details as do the mechanics of reading a paper book and commenting p rivately in the margins. Further, Lanham doesn't ask whether people will continue to want portable paper books for leisure reading in bed or on a beach -- and thus paper and electronic versions of many books will co exist. Despite these limitations, Lanham forcefully opens deep questions about the nature of humanistic inquiry and the relations between readers and authors in a world of electronic writing.

There is a fundamental change in the world of scholarly publishing and libraries as they shift from paper-based to electronic formats. Today, few prolific academic authors peck away at typewriters. While virtually all academic journals articles and books are now produced in electronic form, the majority are sooner or later printed on paper for sale or distribution to their readers. It is difficult to create forums for lively discussion and debates in the paper journals because it can take months from the time that a letter is sent to the editor for it to appear in print. So, most scholarly journals publish research papers, but rarely publish debates about their credibility and importance. These discussions used to take place through correspondence betwee n colleagues and face-to-face at conferences and in special seminars.

The driving images of electronic publishing and digital libraries converge in focussing upon ways that an authors' keystrokes (and thoughts) can be rapidly transmitted to potential readers without the required mediation of paper formats, even if there is significant editorial structuring and filtering. An even richer set of images rests on expanding the scope of scholarly discussion, by using diverse electronic forums to support active dialogues and debates. Today, there are thousands of specialized elect ronic scholarly discussion groups which communicate worldwide through electronic mail via Usenet newsgroups, LISTSERVs, and ad-hoc mailing lists. This trend was heralded by Computer Scientist Peter Denning as a "new paradigm for science" in which b usy scholar could better cope with the torrent of new specialized publications.

One area in which electronic publishing is particularly well organized is high energy physics. Physicists follow work in other labs to build on others' research. But they are also fiercely competitive (Traweek, 1988). Major awards and rewards, such as No bel Prizes and memberships to the National Academy of Sciences, are granted to those who have been the first to be credited with new observations or to develop new theories and paradigms. Like other scientists, physicists circulate early versions of their articles (pre-prints) to colleagues. Because academic publication can take one to two years from the date an article is first submitted to a scholarly journal for publication, physicists who work on a research frontier avidly read their colleagues' prep rints. Hepnet, an electronic database of preprints that is accessible over the Internet, allows high energy physicists to document their claims to fame with preprints unambiguously time-stamped and rapidly accessible world-wide.

"The Electronic Journal: What, Whence, and When?" Ann Okerson argues that electronic journals should become an important form of scholarly communication.

Okerson characterizes Hepnet, whose database of prerints contains over 200,000 hig h energy physics articles, as one of the most interesting experiments in electronic publishing. Physicists also rely upon traditional paper journals to review their pre prints for scientific merit and to publish them in a paper format for circulation to libraries and other subscribers. High-energy physicists publish in both electronic and paper formats, and do it in a way that does not challenge conventional beliefs abou t the legitimacy of paper-based publication.

The electronic journals (e-journals) available through the Internet come closest to fitting the image of direct communication between authors of systematic studies and their readers. In the last few years, electronic journals (e-journals) have appeared i n diverse fields, from avante-garde cultural studies to medicine and even to medieval studies. Okerson's the journal's electronic archives are currently the subject of substantial debate by scholars and librarians. Some scholars, like Anne Okerson, see them as a new form which will bloom in the 21st century. But Oke rson acknowledges that e-journals are criticized for lax intellectual standards and for requiring readers to work with clumsy computer technologies.

For example, some academics assume that article in e-journals are not subject to the kind of stringent peer review that char acterizes the highest quality paper journals. In fact, some journals, in paper or electronic form strictly review each article. Other paper journals and e journals use less restrictive reviews. And to complicate matters, some journals such as the Journal of Artificial Intelligence Research blend e-journal and paper formats by publishing each article electronically when it is accepted, but also publish an single paper issue once a year that librarians (and others) can purchase to file on bookshelves. The Journal of Artificial Intelligence Research doesn't signal its electronic publishing in its name, and it works as a stealth e-journal.

Librarians observe numerous practical problems when academics try to work flexibly with today's e-journals. They might be rapidly disseminated and searched online. But long e-journal articles are hard to read in many common workplaces pla ces unless they are printed on paper. These places include airplane flights, especially during landing and takeoff! More importantly, publishing exclusively in electronic formats has yet to become truly legitimate in major research universities. And few university libraries have explicit collection development policies which enable them to systematically archive specific e-journals.

Library professional Walt Crawford, argues that people who find their news and reading material via the Internet must be specially skeptical about the sources of various files, their authenticity, and their veracity. Crawford, who has served as President of the Library Information Technology Association, is alert to the oppportunities that the Internet opens up and to the complexities of relying upon electronic materials. Traditionally, publishing houses, editors, and librarians acted as gatekeepers, and curators.

Almost any Internet accountholder can set up shop as a publisher, and bypass the institutional apparatus of publishers and librarians to reach a large potential readership. This form of institutional bypass surgery has many charms: it facilitates rapid communication, and it enables authors who have novel viewpoints to reach potentially large audiences. But it assumes that readers are sophisticated enough to make their own judgements of t he veracity of materials.

On March 23, 1989 chemists Martin Fleischmann and B. Stanley Pons announced that they had sustained a cold fusion nuclear reaction at the University of Utah, using relatively simple laboratory apparatus. Almost as noteworthy as their announcement was the way it was made. Rather than following the usual protocol of deferring public discussion until publication of experimental details in a scientific journal, Fleischmann and Pons called a news conference. Within hours scientists world-wide were apprised of the Utah claim, and fax machines and electronic mail networks were soon abuzz with copies of a Fleischmann and Pons paper, which in turn generated hundreds of E-mail responses and discussions of details. I' took several years for the scientific community to conclude that Fleischmann and Pons' experiments and claims were basically not credible. Today, a scientist seeking publicity could promptly announce her results with a web page or a papers sent to a LISTSERV.

More serious, would be the problems of intentional deception. Crawford notes,

> "Anyone with an Internet connection and a decent graphics toolkit can create pages just as impressive as anything from the Library of Congress or NASA--but without any regard for factuality or meaning. You don't even need good taste to build impressive presentations; modern software will provide professional defaults so that you just add your erroneous or misleading text and graphics."

"Information Technology, Scholarship and the Humanities" Vartan Gregorian, President of Brown

University, examines the effects of electronic communication and electronic publishing in terms of the production of knowledg e and teaching in universities. In contrast with Denning he observes that computer nets help academic specialists retain and even refine their narrowness. He argues that,

"We must rise above the obsession with quantity of information and speed of transmission, and recognize that the key issue for us is our ability to organize this information once it has been amassed--to assimilate it, find meaning in it, a nd assure its survival for use by generations to come."

Gregorian notes that specialization has been a master trend in universities for over 100 years. Computers did not cause specialization. But he notes that "Information technologies also contribute to the fragmentation of knowledge by allowing us to organize ourselves into ever-more-specialized communities." Gregorian makes some rather harsh observations about electronic communities in academic specialties:

Are you developing an interest in exotic insects, rare minerals, or an obscure poet? With little effort you can use electronic mail and conferencing to find several others, in Japan, Peru, or Bulgaria, with whom you can communicate every d ay, creating your own small, self-confirming world of theory, technique, and methodology. McLuhan's prediction that electronic communication would create a global village is wrong, in my opinion. What is being created is less like a village than an e ntity that reproduces the worst aspects of urban life: the ability to retreat into small communities of the likeminded, safe not only from unnecessary interactions with those whose ideas and attitudes are not like our own, but safe from having to rel ate our interests and results to other communities.

Gregorian's harsh criticisms would be most apt when scholars (and other professionals) work primarily on-line from their homes or offices. And some faculty do adopt these hermit-like workstyles. But universities also create face-to-face forums that bring together people with diverse viewpoints -- invited speakers, committees to create or review curricula, interdisciplianry research institutes, faculty seminars, and so on. Gregorian's dark vision is an interesting warning. But it may also be a byprduct of university administrations that reward extreme specialization, and that don't develop lively forums and formats for discussions amongst their faculty. In those cases, a special risk for urban universities with dispersed faculty, life on-line may become mu ch more seductive than life on-campus.

When Do Electronic Forums Computer Enhance or Undermine Community Life ?

"On the Road Again" Richard Sclove and Jeffrey Scheuer examine the metaphor of information highways by discussing the social effects of the Interstate Highway system on community life in the United States. Sclove and Scheuer not e that the interstate highways were not constructed because the public demanded them. Rather, a coalition of powerful business firms lobbied Congress to create them. Although they expanded Americans' sense of the open road and space to roam, they were s ometimes routed through cities in ways that divided neighborhoods. They became the gateways to regional shopping malls that killed many lively downtowns.

Today, interstates are clogged with commuter traffic during urban rush hours.

Electronic services might also compete with today's public places, if only because few people can (or will) simultaneously log in to an on-line service while simultaneously participating in a face to face group meeting outside their homes. If the enthusiasts for electronic communities and virtual communities had their visions come true, electronic services would be so active they could shrivel many existing traditional face to face forums. They would be like the lively regional mall drawing trade away fr om the old down-town.

Bibliography

Arms, Caroline, *Campus strategies for libraries and electronic information*, Bedford, Mass., Digital Press, 1990.

Ayres Robert and Steven Miller, "Robotics, CAM and Industrial Productivity," *National Productivity Review*, Winter 1981-2.

Barr A., Cohen P. R. and Feigenbaum E. A., *The Handbook of Artificial Intelligence*, 3 vols. Kaufmann, Los Altos, CA, 1981.

Braun Ludwig, "Computer-aided learning and the Microcomputer Revolution", *Programmed Learning and Educational Technology*, vol. 18, No. 4, 1981.

Brindley, L.J. (ed.), 'The electronic campus: an information strategy', *Library and information research report 73*, London, British Library, 1989.

Computer-Based National Information Systems: Technology and Public Policy Issues Office of Technology Assessment, US Congress, Washington, DC, 1981.

Daniel, Evelyn, 'Information resources and organisational structure', *Journal of the American Society for Information Science*, 1983.

Davis Dwight B., "Supercomputers: A Strategic Imperative?" *High Technology*, May 1984.

Davis Ruth M., "Computers and Electronics for Individual Services", *Science*, February 12, 1982.

Dray James and Joseph A. Menosky, "Computers and a New World Order", *Technology Review*, May-June 1983.

Glossbrenner Alfred, *The Complete Handbook of Personal Computer Communications: Everything You Need to Go Online With the World*, St. Martins Press, New York, 1983.

Halevi G., *The Role of Computers in Manufacturing Processes*, John Wiley, New York, 1982.

Kahin, Brian, *Building information infrastructure: issue in the development of the National Research and Education Network*, London, McGraw-Hill, 1992.

Leone Robert A. and Stephen P. Bradley, "Toward an Effective Industrial Policy", *Harvard Business Review*, November-December 1981.

Malamud, Carl, *Exploring the Internet: a technical travelogue*, London, Prentice-Hall, 1992.

Mandeville Thomas, "The Spatial Effects of Information Technology", *Futures*, February 1983. A review of the literature on possible urban / regional problems.

Orvell Miles, "The Screen Revolution", *Technology Review*, February-March, 1982. A look at McLuhan's writings in the light of new developments.

Parsons, G. L. 'Information technology: a new competitive weapon', *Sloan Management Review*, Autumn 1983.

Rada, J. (1980). *The Impact of Microelectronics* Geneva, chap. 7.

Work, Colin, 'The future development of campus-wide information systems: towards the virtual campus', *Journal of Information Networking* 1(1), 1993.

Index